LIFE, AFTER

Also by Antoine Leiris

You Will Not Have My Hate

Antoine Leiris

LIFE, AFTER

Translated from the French
by Sam Taylor

Harvill Secker
LONDON

1 3 5 7 9 10 8 6 4 2

Harvill Secker, an imprint of Vintage, is part of the
Penguin Random House group of companies whose addresses can be
found at global.penguinrandomhouse.com

Penguin
Random House
UK

First published by Harvill Secker in 2022
First published with the title *La vie, après* by
Éditions Robert Laffont in France in 2019

A CIP catalogue record for this book is available from
the British Library

penguin.co.uk/vintage

ISBN 9781787302631

Typeset in 11.85/16.75 pt Fournier MT Std
by Integra Software Services Pvt. Ltd, Pondicherry

Printed and bound in Great Britain by Clays Ltd, Elcograf S.p.A.

The authorised representative in the EEA is Penguin Random House

'We [...] were, so to speak, the end of a lineage [...]. One might have thought that we didn't exist, that characters – invisible but much more important than us – were continuing to fill the mirrors of our house with their images. I would prefer to avoid even the suspicion of hyperbole, particularly at the end of a sentence, but one might say, in a way, that in old families, it is the living who seem to be shadows of the dead.'

Marguerite Yourcenar, *Alexis*

'Whoever wishes to remember must surrender to forgetfulness, to the risk of absolute oblivion and to that beautiful randomness which then becomes memory.'

Maurice Blanchot, *The Book to Come*

FOREWORD

I wrote my first book during the strangest and most violent moment of my life. My wife, Hélène, had just been killed in the terrorist attacks at the Bataclan, on 13 November 2015.

In *You Will Not Have My Hate*, I described the days following her death, which I lived through with our son Melvil, who was seventeen months old at the time.

On several occasions since then, I have attempted to write again. At first, I tried fiction. I wanted to tell a story that wasn't mine, with invented characters and places. A real novel.

I spent months working on this, before resigning myself to the fact that it was beyond my capabilities. My imagination was wholly focused on the invention of our new life. I couldn't conceive of anything beyond that necessity: saving us, creating spaces where we could live, and inhabiting them. Existing.

I threw away all those pages and gave myself the time to live.

Grief is a succession of transformations. You slough off your old skins, one by one. You constantly change. This is what time does to everybody, in normal circumstances. But in this particular case, the changes happened more quickly.

Four years later, I can safely say that I am no longer the same man. The same is true for Melvil, of course. He isn't a baby any more, but a happy little boy.

During those years, he passed from silence and babbling to words and language. He has grown up so quickly.

I waited until we were on a solid footing before I started writing again. Then I tried to record those metamorphoses, the tides of change that have transformed us since our world vanished in a mist, up to the moment when – almost suddenly – the sky clears.

That is when it begins. Life, after.

So this book is not about ten days, but about four long years, during which I learned so much. I have tried to describe daily routines and special moments, to recount how I learned to become a father, to live with ghosts, to listen to them, and to accept this paper-thin gap between life and death.

Today, we are happy and free. Free of our past, and strengthened by our past.

Melvil and I have rediscovered meaning and pleasure in existence. So I wanted to write again, but nothing more than that. Just to write. In the first person.

About myself, Antoine Leiris: a son, a brother, a father. And about the strange and wonderful 'us' that my son and I form together.

1

It is the year *after*, in the middle of summer. I drop him at his grandmother's house so I won't have him under my feet. I kiss him the way I eat marshmallows – unable to stop, stuffing myself until I feel sick.

I leave him, but I wish I could keep him close to me. Those marshmallow kisses lie heavy on my stomach.

In the first line, I wrote: 'the year *after*'. Rereading this, I realise that my language has changed. Now, I say 'before' or 'after', the way people talk about before or after the fall of the Berlin Wall, before or after the Second World War, before or after the invention of printing, before or after Jesus Christ. It is the tipping point of our story.

I never wrote: 'Hélène's death'. I don't say it, and even writing it now feels wrong. I just vaguely locate periods of time by specifying 'before' or 'after'.

I understand how brutal and reductive this is. My way of avoiding the obstacle while recognising that it's impossible.

So, it is the year *after*, in the middle of summer. Like a burglar, I have planned to act in silence and in darkness. No music, no light, nothing to enhance the moment.

At home, I wait until it is completely dark outside. I look through the window: dust falling onto the street below. A dense dampness starts to rise from the white-hot tarmac, like a body standing, stripping off, an arousing and afflicting body.

It's nearly time.

I open a bottle of Rully – white wine has enough sulphites to allow me to forget the coming evening – and sit on the floor with my glass.

I gave myself one night to attempt to do things 'right'. To avoid the obstacle again.

But it's obvious that I'm lying to myself: it won't be enough. I'll have to be quick if I want to be finished by morning. Impossible to do it 'right' with so little time. Impossible to do it 'right' with so little desire.

I have to accomplish in a few hours what I have been putting off for months: to sort through all her things, to face up to the real shape of grief. The apartment feels like it's flooded. With water, a continuous body of liquid, pouring through, filling the cracks, spreading over the surface.

Our apartment is intact; exactly as it was before. Nothing has moved since last year.

As teenagers, we would sometimes play this game: 'If you had to take three films to a desert island, which ones would you choose?' A younger me would have said, without hesitation: *2001: A Space Odyssey*, so that I could understand the final scene at last; *The Verdict*, because of Paul Newman; and *Quai des Orfèvres*, so I could once again hear Louis Jouvet's curt, husky voice.

Today, the question could be asked in different ways.

'If you had to take three objects to remind you of that life, which ones would you choose?'

'If you had to take three objects so that your son would understand what that life was like, which ones would you choose?'

Being an adult means thinking for Melvil as well as myself. Before, I was used to making important decisions only for myself, not for two people.

I wish someone could advise me, could tell me: in ten years, your son will be glad to possess that. In twenty, you'll need this. In fifty, you'll love looking at that object.

But I must act alone. And then I must accept responsibility for my choices.

I must stop the love of a whole lifetime at the moment when it broke. Then break it apart into images and instants. Categorise them and tidy them into little boxes, where they can live once again.

Create another space for them, for her. Imagine her fully, breathing in the vanished present, the drowned continent.

*

I am not attached to things. I am indifferent to ownership. Possessions are an encumbrance. I have never accumulated objects. I am not a collector. I am not trying to amass an inheritance, just write a story.

I have never kept anything of my past lives. I belong to one of those families whose histories are not engraved in stone. As a young child, I remember envying people who could boast a lineage, a past beyond their own. Anyone with an accent, a culture, a colour, a geography, something that distinguished them from others and that they carried around with them like a shell.

We had none of that, so even the smallest detail seemed extraordinary to me.

Friends would tell me about staying in the countryside, at their grandparents' house, walking by the seaside, going out in a boat, and I would imagine epic adventures, exotic tales, perfect happiness.

My most vivid memory of a childhood holiday was in the mountains. A friend had invited me to their family's cabin, one week in summer. We went hiking and his father told me I climbed like a goat.

I drank water straight from the river. I cut my bread with an Opinel knife. I felt I belonged to that story. I was a mountain-dweller. It had run through my veins for generations.

Later, though, I repeated the family trait: I kept nothing. Or almost nothing.

I spent my life throwing everything away and starting over. I left houses and lived in others, my only legacy an empty space and the promise of a new life.

But now our apartment is like a museum. I think about Pablo Neruda's house, at Isla Negra, west of Santiago, on Chile's Pacific coast, where he is buried with his wife Matilde.

The building, a refuge in stone and wood, is just as it was when they lived there together, and the objects that filled it are still in the same places – ship figureheads, seashells, a wooden horse from a carousel.

In the poet's study, everything is pure, just like 'before'. The space is enormous, the large bookcase facing the ocean still covered with objects. Some say that, observing his armchair, they felt their heart thrum, as when you think you see a shadow flit past or sense the presence of a ghost in a heavier mass of air.

Objects belonging to someone who dies immediately become sacred. They are relics, proof that those who were no longer are, that they had a life of their own. That she had a life of her own. That she had her own secrets and fears, that she kept her keys in her trouser pockets, that she wore those necklaces around her neck or tied the ribbons of those sandals around her ankles.

They are links between here and there, where the living still linger for a while. In details, in vestiges, like the traces of lost civilisations.

I feel unsteady. I am doing what I always did before, but this time with the sensation that I am transgressing on intimate secrets.

I am both guardian and thief. He who preserves and he who destroys. Violator and violated.

Cardboard boxes are piled up in front of me. Emptied cupboards and drawers stand looking at useless objects scattered across the floor.

At the foot of a television stand, containing a TV set that I haven't watched in at least a year, there is a box filled with chargers of all shapes and sizes that I have never managed to throw away.

It is almost the only thing that has followed me from the rundown flat on the periphery of Paris that I shared with a friend as a twenty-year-old to this one-bedroom apartment in the fifteenth arrondissement, where we had moved recently. It was practical. There were childcare centres and gardens nearby. And we felt good here.

Yet it's probably the saddest part of Paris. It's not pretty, and it's not full of life. The neighbourhood falls asleep at nine in the evening and is woken by the sound of school bells. Rebuilt after the war, it is dominated by the architecture of its large apartment buildings and the lifestyle that comes with them. People live there, they go shopping, go for walks on Sundays, have children, grow old, die, and that's all.

I keep our past in Montmartre inside me like a precious snow globe. To remember, I just have to look through the glass: life, street peddlers, voices from the bar below.

Melvil's first months with us in our bedroom. Short nights and summer sun. The day we moved, I hid one of his dummies under the bathtub. As a way of saying 'we were here', leaving something of us behind.

*

The Rully doesn't help. Everything I do feels like a sacrilege. I start trembling when I find her school notebooks. I touch her handwriting with my fingertip. It's a girl's handwriting, neat and pretty. The loops of her *l*s are perfect. The dots over her *i*s are perfect circles.

In another box, I find photographs of her. One of her naked body, taken a few weeks after we met. Tattoos of swallows on her skin. I remember the feel of her breast in my hand, the perfection of her figure, the softness of her curves.

In an instant, I feel her weight, her lightness, her fullness, and I embrace her. Remembering that buried sensuality: her breasts were where our skin touched. Where my longing met her yearning.

All night long, I desecrate her drawers. I unwrap packages, tear open envelopes, empty jars of make-up. I speed up. I throw stuff away without thinking, especially stuff I haven't seen before.

I keep the things she used most often. Her phone – which I have never opened, afraid of violating her secrets, finding evidence of infidelity or boredom. It belonged to her, not me.

In the box where I keep my wedding ring, I put all the jewellery that she wore. I keep the contents of her bedside table and a picture of us, cheeks red in the London cold.

Then I think about the logistics, about all the possible organisation methods: I could categorise her relics according to where they were kept, or which period of her life they belonged to, or their usefulness, or their value. I could do it properly, in a logical, ordered way.

Instead of which, I just toss everything randomly into cardboard boxes and seal them up. When each box is full, I write on it, in black felt-tip pen: 'Hélène'. As if death had left her only one word, a name.

The sun rises. I have slept barely three hours. I step out of the shower. My hair is wet and plastered to my head, there's a towel around my waist.

Under its grey veil, Paris looks apocalyptic. No light pierces the gloom; the horizon seals the greyness in. Soon it will explode in a cascade of orange beams.

My brother comes to pick up the boxes. I have to do it quickly, leave myself no time for choice. Throw them all in the back of his van, in no particular order. Hurry upstairs and carry more boxes down. Break my back to rid myself of this headache. Don't think about it any more. Leave.

I unload everything in the new apartment. I organise Melvil's bedroom first, then the living room and my bedroom.

I want everything to be ready for his arrival. I want it to feel alive. I have told him that this is going to be an adventure.

I try to make everything seem like an adventure. We're like those orphans in stories, like two Rémis from Hector Malot's book, seeking out the next part of their journey.

We spend our days navigating the Zambezi and climbing in the Himalayas. When we go to my sister's house, it's the Yellow Expedition: we are putting our lives in peril, crossing into uncharted territory.

We fear the natives, with their unfamiliar habits. We face up to wild animals in collars, packs of canines with tennis balls in their mouths, felines crouching on windowsills, waiting to pounce on their prey, giant insects that are perhaps carriers of terrible diseases.

We invade the outside world, exposing ourselves to its dangers.

*

Our new apartment, on the sixth floor of a modern building, is the next undiscovered land. Today's adventure begins at ground level, in the middle of this straight grey street.

There are no shops and very little traffic. The street becomes livelier in the mornings, lunchtimes and afternoons, when the local school opens its doors. The air is filled with the sound of children for a few minutes, and then silence falls again.

Our apartment building is brand new, all mod cons. Before, I would have hated it. I liked old stone buildings, their beauty and their history. The idea of a before-us and an after-us, of our time being part of a greater whole.

But I am coming round to the benefits of the modern, the individual, the new, the ready-made. No *before*s of any kind. I am embracing the now, the immediate, the convenient, the practical, the ephemeral, the washable, the soundproofed, this brave new world of straight lines and white walls.

I like being ready to leave, in permanent motion.

Unlike with old buildings, the stairwell here is not in the centre. In the evenings, you can't hear anything: no lovers rushing home to their bedrooms, no drunken partygoers trying to open the wrong door. In the mornings, you can't hear the children hurtling downstairs to get to school on time.

Our staircase is only used as an emergency exit. We take the lift, as long as it's not out of order. Just like everybody else.

In the common areas, the floor is linoleum. It sounds like hospitals: it hisses when you walk on it. The light is white. The concierge told me that the apartments' front doors had recently been painted red. But the tenants complained, so all the doors were painted sea-blue again.

And yet the architects did allow themselves a few liberties, as if to make people forget the sad regularity of their surroundings. Like that decorative metal structure with holes in it that stands on our balcony and on the balconies of the three floors above us.

It's a strange, rounded shape, like the sail of a ship. Perfect for a voyage.

I wanted to take the first step alone. Like a guide scouting the terrain, testing the depth of the water, checking that the ice is thick enough, that the knot in the rope won't slip. Now, I can show him.

Once the apartment is in order, I go to pick up Melvil from my mother-in-law's house. I take her a cardboard box filled with things from the old apartment. I give her back her daughter but keep my wife. They are two people now and never again will they be the same. They will each exist independently of the other in the stories that we tell about them.

They won't have the same character, the same beauty, or even the same surname.

They won't dress in the same way or talk about the same subjects. They won't speak in the same voice or use the same words. They won't have been born on the same day. But they will have died at the same moment, in the same place.

Melvil leaps into my arms. A leap of faith. He takes a good run-up, throws himself headlong into the void, surrendering to fate. I am simultaneously the leaping child and the arms that catch him.

Smiling at him like someone who has passed an exam and is now expecting to be congratulated, I say: 'Let's go to the new house.'

He holds my hand. On the way there, I have time to get him excited about this move. To make him happy, to ward off the shadows of disappointment, doubt, uncertainty.

I tell him about the room with his toys in it. The new living room. I bought a little table just for him. He'll be able to draw pictures and eat his afternoon snack there.

In the lift, I pick him up so he can reach the button. He thinks this is fun. He smiles.

We go inside and I show him the rooms, one by one. I fear he won't like it, that he'll say it's not right for us, that it's too angular, too boring, too precise. Too much concrete for a home.

He is silent, like a kitten sniffing a bowl of milk for a long time before it starts to drink. I open the door to his bedroom. At last, happiness overcomes him. The joy of familiarity. He dives on his box of toy cars.

Without a word, I go into the living room and sit on the sofa. I want to give him time to settle in. The feeling of apprehension hasn't completely left me. I will understand later that it is never really going to leave me.

*

A few minutes pass. I hear his footsteps coming this way. He stands next to me and tells me he'd like to go out. Of course: he wants to go outside, to explore.

'So do you like your new home?' I ask.

'Yes.'

'Good. Let's go then.'

He smiles. We go outside. The simple happiness of children. I think, we're better off outside than inside.

We stay out until evening. I put him to bed in his new room, in his old bed. As I turn out the light, I say: 'Don't worry. This new house is just for sleeping.'

2

October 2016

Our bedrooms are exactly the same size. And we each have our toys.

For me, they're some old watches with brand names that have vanished and been resurrected, names that evoke France's industrial past – Lip, Yema, Baltic, Jaz.

I put them carefully away in their box and wear them according to the circumstances. Rallygraf, Aquascaphe, Nautic-Ski, Jazistor. The promise of so many adventures around my wrist.

For Melvil, it's a mountain of cars, figures made from plastic or playdough. He has enough construction equipment to make any building-site foreman green with envy.

I spent hours on the Internet, choosing the best models for him. It was an odyssey of consumption. I read lots of blogs and customer reviews, before identifying a Japanese brand that produces the most faithful (and expensive) replicas. I buy them in bulk, for my own pleasure as much as his.

I am six years old, with an adult's salary, and I want the whole toy shop. I come home with my arms full of packages and lie on my bedroom floor to play with them. I can spend hours doing that. Days. My father calls me for dinner.

The first weekends after the move, we spent in furniture shops, seeking out replacements for items that didn't suit the new apartment and trying to fill the emptiness created by the extra space.

I wanted the place to feel lived-in. I wanted it to be home. I thought that would be good for a father and his son. I thought about those divorced men who have to furnish their new apartments so their children can visit them: the furnishings have to tell a comforting story – 'Papa is fine', 'You'll be happy here'.

So I hung pictures of us on the walls. I didn't feel brave enough to sort through all the boxes again – I just took the ones from the top of the pile. Among the photographs I found, there were images of our first date, our travels, our birthdays, our wedding and Melvil's birth.

I picked up one of the rare ones showing all three of us, at a childcare centre party. Melvil still has a dummy hanging from his sweater. He's chubby. Around his lips, there are smears of the chocolate cake we made. When the party is over, we will go to the park to enjoy the good weather.

In another picture, he's on his mother's shoulders, one morning on our way to the market. She is determined to make apple sauce that he will stubbornly refuse to eat.

There is also the photograph that we took of us in a boat at the Jardin d'Acclimatation. I have my hand around his shoulder and he looks fearful as he nuzzles against me, as if the camera might eat him.

One last image shows my little brother, my big sister and myself as children. My brother is in the middle, in a canary-yellow polo shirt, flanked by two big toothless grins.

*

I also hung a few unremarkable paintings that Hélène inherited from her father: Dutch landscapes, where the calmness of the scenery contrasts with the anxiety of the viewer, alone facing that emptiness.

There are record covers on the bookcase, although I never listen to the discs inside any more, since I don't have a turntable. Lou Reed in dark sunglasses that can't hide the sadness he feels at Sally's inability to dance; the Rolling Stones's *Sticky Fingers*, with the zip sewn onto the sleeve; *Nashville Skyline*, containing one of our favourite songs: 'Girl from the North Country', sung by Bob Dylan and Johnny Cash. Another journey.

Boxes full of books are piled up everywhere. There's a sofa, which is now striped with felt-tip marks and flecked with melted chocolate stains. And then there's my brown leather armchair – 'Papa's seat'.

I filled it. I filled the walls and other spaces because I was afraid of emptiness. And also because I was afraid of other people and how they might judge us, judge me.

I was afraid they would discover my helplessness in the set-up of this apartment, that they would sniff out my inability to lead this family alone.

Those decorations reassured me. Anyone who visits now will see that we are still alive, that we are occupying the premises. We are not lacking in anything, or anyone.

I filled the frame and I pushed everything else off-camera. I didn't know what to do with it.

On the day we move, the things from before are stored in cellars, at my brother's apartment, my sister's apartment, or in the second basement beneath our feet, in a room too small to fit everything, at the end of a long corridor, last door on the left. It is eight floors below us, but the memories it holds are so important that I feel as if they are just beneath our feet.

Off-camera means: out of sight but close by. It's there – we know it even without seeing it. It's there – we just don't know where to put it yet. And it lives, beyond us.

One day, a few weeks after we moved in, I couldn't help myself. I went downstairs, unfastened the padlock, and left the door ajar to see what would happen: if someone would go inside, or leave, if anything might occur without me having to make a decision.

The next day, when I went back, the padlock was fastened again. I put my ear to the door and listened for something moving around inside. A mouse scurried between my feet and flattened its body to get under the door.

I jumped, and felt stupid. What had I been expecting? Something magical? To wake up from a nightmare and discover the cellar emptied, all her belongings neatly stowed away somewhere else?

I didn't want to open the door. I felt like a trespasser. I had the impression that someone lived there now. This space – close enough not to be completely unfamiliar, distant enough to be forgotten – belongs to Hélène.

Her memory left our old apartment and now it resides in these boxes. The space is hers. We can visit her. What's sacred is beneath our feet.

Melvil and I are not afraid of cellars or attics. What scares other people piques our curiosity. We share the same obsession: searching. We like the cloud of dust that rises, the spider that runs away when we lift a lid.

During the first months, whenever I go down to the basement, Melvil demands to come with me. We put some other furniture in there, but we don't touch her belongings. We build the pile higher. We add layers. We clear out the passing time. The seasons. In summer, we put away the winter clothes that are now too small. In winter, we put away the summer clothes. We throw out whatever we don't need.

For his third birthday, Melvil's cot is replaced by a real bed. So the cot goes down to the basement.

I open the cellar door. I assess how much is in there and how much space remains. There's not enough. That little room is growing cramped.

I could have taken a day off. I could have opened all the boxes and gone through them. I could also have got rid of the cot. Or simply disassembled it.

Instead of that, I suddenly take hold of the cardboard boxes filled with Hélène's clothes and remove them from the tiny space in which they've been stored. I feel as if someone else is doing this, not me. I would like to keep all of it, as it is, even if I know I have to make space. We can't go back to the beginning of our story every time we want to turn a page of the book.

I hesitate for a moment and finally decide to keep her wedding dress, another one with flowers on it that made her look like a Rohmer heroine, and the leather jacket she was wearing that night.

All the rest, I throw away without giving myself time to think about it. I feel as though I am taking something that no longer belongs to me. The letters, the photographs, the clothes ... they were the new body that death gave Hélène. A body made of objects, cloth and paper, plastic and glass. A scattered body that I am now tearing to pieces so I can rid myself of it.

I didn't cry. I would have time to regret it later. I made the choice despite myself. I made the choice for Melvil. I chose to let the layers of memories settle and compact.

That's how it is: nobody ditches their entire life story in one go. You throw it away little by little, whenever you need to make more space, giving yourself just enough time to feel the emotions on each occasion.

In this way, the story is transformed, ceasing to be a simple timeline where events and objects can be neatly located. It becomes instead this paradoxical whole, from which only the most significant feelings emerge. Love. Loss. Fragments. Smells. Moments.

Exhausted and relieved, I contemplate the new empty space like a man who's just washed all the dishes in the sink, then fill it with the wooden cot. I put everything into big black bin liners and haul them up to our apartment with the sensation of having taken a step forward.

I don't want to give her things away or leave them in a skip for scavengers. I prefer to know that they've vanished somewhere. I don't want anyone else to have these pieces of her.

Late that afternoon, I pick up Melvil from day care. I take him home and he sees the black plastic bags without saying anything. I tell him we're going to carry them downstairs. I grab one. He imitates me, picking up the smallest one. We fill our arms.

Out on the street, we stand up straight. The bin lorry will be here soon. Like all kids his age, Melvil is fascinated by those huge vehicles. The noises they make. The ballet around them.

Two green men jump from the running board at the back of the lorry. They see us and smile at Melvil. There's a strange complicity between my son and these men. I throw in the first bag, then Melvil – happy and proud to be working alongside his father – helps me carry the rest over there.

I feel as if he knows, even if he doesn't understand. Or maybe that's not the point. He's just happy to be doing what I do. It's the meaning of this connection, paternity. Letting him follow in my footsteps. His father's footsteps.

The two binmen congratulate him. Melvil, standing on the pavement in his pyjamas and slippers, raises his hand to wave at them.

The lorry sets off again with its cloth coffin.

It's over.

Her belongings have left. One day, I know, he'll ask me why we got rid of it all. At that moment, I will undoubtedly regret this decision, but I'll be able to explain why I did it: to free him from the weight of those objects so that he can cherish what he knew and felt.

We can now weave a legend around their departure. Tell anecdotes about them, even if they're not true. We can give those objects whatever beauty we want them to have.

We can bestow on them the everlasting power of fantasy, and we can live with that power.

We head back to our ship's sail. Melvil goes to his bedroom to look at books. In the kitchen, I get dinner ready.

He returns, wearing his silly face. He runs through the corridor and stands in front of me, leaning slightly forward, feet nailed to the floor, hands joined at his chest, head raised. There's a prank in his head and he can't wait to release it.

'What's your name?' he asks me. I lean down towards him and show him my puzzled frown. This is exactly what he was hoping for. I can sense his excitement growing. He's finding it hard to keep the colony of ladybirds inside his mouth. He starts hopping about as those little beetles tickle his palate.

A swarm of red and black dots flies up at me as he laughs and shouts: 'You're Geppetto!'

I don't understand.

He hops into his room. Well, I say he hops, but it's possible he runs or skips or dances his way there. Because, like all kids his age, Melvil has lost the ability to walk. He moves only in arabesques.

He comes back holding a book. Before leaving him for a six-month internship, his nanny – 'Alessandra number two' as he calls her, since his first nanny was also called Alessandra – gave him her favourite story from her Italian childhood. *The Adventures of Pinocchio* by Carlo Collodi, which he offers to me, arms outstretched, back straight and feet together, as if it were some sacred object.

His smile is so big, it looks like it might spill over the sides of his face.

He asks: 'And what will you call me?'

I still don't understand. He takes my hand and leads me to my armchair. I sit down and he nestles in the tiny space between my body and the armrest.

He points at the book.

'Once upon a time, there was a piece of wood. It was not an expensive piece of wood. Far from it. Just a common block of firewood, one of those thick, solid logs that are put on the fire in winter to make cold rooms cosy and warm. A piece of wood that wept and laughed like a child.'

He starts wriggling around when the piece of wood tells the carpenter that his plane is tickling it.

His body stiffens as we approach the moment he's been waiting for.

'As soon as he reached home, Geppetto took his tools and began to cut and shape the wood into a marionette. "What shall I call him?" he said to himself.'

I don't have time to finish my sentence before he explodes with joy.

'And what will you call me?' I still don't understand what he wants me to say, but I can sense that it's important I don't want to get the wrong end of the stick because that could ruin his enjoyment.

I pretend I haven't heard his question. I continue reading, while thinking about his question.

'"What shall I call him?" wondered Geppetto. "I think I'll call him Pinocchio."'

As soon as the word is out of my mouth, Melvil throws himself at me and starts twisting my arms in all directions, like one of those clowns who turn balloons into animals.

After only a few seconds, I have a miniature poodle at the end of my shoulder. He jumps onto my leg like a horse leaping a fence, in slow motion. Then he sits there, face looking at me, his body swaddled in my arm.

It is at this point that I notice the illustration in the book. Melvil is in exactly the same pose as the little wooden marionette in his maker's arms.

Laughing, he says to me again: 'What's your name?'

At last I understand. Papa is always a bit slow.

To make him happy, I say that my name is Geppetto.

His eyes are like the Paris sky on the night of 14 July.

'And what will you call me?' In my best Italian accent, I tell him that I will call him Pinocchio.

This child is mine, I think, and I am his father. Suddenly I want to hug him tight, but he has already escaped and is laughing loudly, repeating the magic words: 'I will call you Pinocchio!'

*

I see him being born again. That strange, foreign body. Viscous and bloody. A son of love and beauty.

His wails aren't loud enough. It's nothing to worry about, but they take him to the room next door. The midwives invite me to accompany them. Hélène gestures for me to go.

They put him on a small table above a heat lamp. They make him climb an imaginary staircase, bending his knees. They say something in Latin to explain why it's normal that tar is coming out of my son's bottom. Then they touch his testicles and the reaction is instant. 'At least we know *that's* working,' they say.

He's turned around and upside down. The midwives handle him like a butcher with a piece of stewing meat: with dexterity and love. Their aprons are stained with blood. My little roast is tied up with string.

Then there's a silence. A doctor has told me that my son is fine and everybody has suddenly left the room. I am alone with that little bundle of flesh and big dark eyes.

He is lying there in front of me and I don't know if I'm allowed to touch him. The midwives didn't say anything. I don't know what to say to him. I don't know what to think. He's lying there as though he's always been there but I just never noticed before. He is there.

And he is still there. Next to me now. He's come back to ask me to read the rest of the story.

I pick up where I left off. 'After choosing the name for his marionette, Geppetto set seriously to work to make the hair, the forehead, the eyes. Fancy his surprise when he noticed that these eyes moved and then stared fixedly at him.'

I feel him relax.

My little piece of wood with his round sculpted eyes falls asleep. He falls asleep in his plastic box with its orange light.

'Geppetto continued to work. When he'd finished, he took hold of the marionette under the arms and put him on the floor to teach him to walk. But Pinocchio's legs were so stiff that he could not move them, so Geppetto held his hand and showed him how to put one foot in front of the other.'

A few lines that are like our life. His first steps, his stiff legs, falling, standing up again, learning to put one foot in front of the other.

3

May 2017

We have our routine. It traces the borders of our space, gives each of us a rhythm and a role. The routine is a place where we feel happy, safe, cocooned. Habit is comfortable; no expectations means no disappointments.

Since the day after, this is what I have clung to. It is the only thing I can get a grip on, a lifebelt in the ocean. Organising each day, setting up simple rules, always on time, everything in its place. Above all, don't let anything unexpected happen.

With the aid of this routine, I do what I didn't think myself capable of doing. I run our household.

*

To begin with, it is a response to anxiety. A structure to stop us falling. Building a framework to shelter us. Doing things 'right'.

Over time, I learn to enjoy the slightest variations. It is pleasure without risk, literature without an author, wine without drunkenness. Our days advance, task after task, and when each one is done, we can look back at its perfect completion.

I schedule every moment of the day. Some are immutable – waking up, going to bed, meals, day care. Others can evolve, depending on the objectives that I have drawn up and the bigger picture of our pace of life, which I plan over a whole week – physical activities, writing, games, relaxation.

Even the free spaces have strict borders.

As a father, I tick all the boxes because I am afraid of emptiness. I organise outings, I buy his clothes in advance, I register for everything on time, I clean the apartment every day.

Through repetition, I become an expert at housework, laundry in particular. Every day, I discover subtle new nuances to this art.

I already knew that I had to separate whites and colours, put each product in its own special tray and not directly into the machine itself, but that was the limit of my knowledge. My only ambition was to make the clothes clean.

This lack of expertise inevitably led to calamity. One day, a bib that couldn't decide if it was crimson or blood-orange chose to bleed out in a machine full of whites.

All Melvil's T-shirts, his little wool jumper with buttons on the collar, his bath towel … they all turned the colour of smoked salmon. The same colour that you see piled up on French supermarket shelves just before Christmas. Midway between pink and orange, with thin white stripes. The colour of failure.

It was only the laundry that lost its purity, and yet my entire equilibrium was washed out. When I saw those ruined clothes, I felt so devastated that I didn't think I'd ever recover.

It was proof of my helplessness, my incompetence as a father. Everything would always be too much, the burden too heavy for me to carry. I would win no victories and my defeats would be bloody, crushing, bitter, the battlefields inside me.

I had to face this anguish alone. The only way I could deal with it was by being methodical and determined. So I started again at square one, establishing a clear strategy and committing all my strength to its implementation.

First, I read the forums to find out what brands of washing powder were best for young children. I found one that claimed to have capsules with magical properties, promising a journey of the senses through a landscape that resembled the Swiss Alps.

To that, I added an antiseptic stain remover that eliminated 99.9% of bacteria, although there was no mention of what that 0.1% consisted of. Bacteria beyond the powers of any cleaning product, presumably.

To me, that 0.1% of invincible bacteria represented, with scientific sharpness, the way fatherhood felt. There is always something left to do. You can never tick all the boxes. Every time, you have to start all over again. And even after that, there are still at least 0.1% of problems that remain unresolved.

Next, I read the user's manual for my washing machine. There, I learned many things: those devices are much more complex than you'd think. For wool, handwash in cold water and be careful to spread the item out on a flat surface afterwards or it could end up misshapen. Cotton: 40°C is the usual selection, but it can be raised to 60°C for whites and sheets. Coats, cuddly toys and anything fragile should be washed on a 'delicate' cycle.

A tumble dryer leaves clothes feeling rough and wears them out prematurely, so it's better to dry them on a line.

But that isn't as simple as you'd think either. You have to leave the washing out long enough that it dries thoroughly and the smell of damp is eliminated, but not so long that it gets dusty.

I continued improving my techniques by working on clothing rotation. Whenever I have nearly enough white items to do a wash, I dress my son as an angel: white underpants, white T-shirt, white socks. If that's not sufficient, then a bath towel can never be clean enough.

I wound up loving the sight of clean laundry hanging out to dry. The drying rack is always open and always full. It is an infinite source of satisfaction.

I let these little victories intoxicate me. I work, I look after Melvil, and I take care of our apartment.

I don't want to think about or do anything else. I want to be this man, to define myself this way. I want others to define me this way too. I want to be known for my usefulness.

So I add more and more tasks to my weekly schedule. Laundry, shopping, cooking. Cleaning windows, tidying bedrooms. All of this forms a protective wall around our life. Meanwhile, life goes on putting spokes in my wheel and sneering as I fall on my face.

This life that was thrust upon me. This life that I must handle on my own.

And that is what I do: I handle it. I construct a square life, with no alarms and no surprises. Existence has to lose its presence, its spontaneity. It becomes artificial, built out of tips I've picked up from parenting guides and scenes I've witnessed at my sister's house.

It must be tender and organised. A show home that you visit and admire for its reassuring orderliness. I don't want to have to worry about designing or building this house – I want it ready to live in now. A turnkey life.

I have to be two people at once. Father and mother. Since this is impossible, I must be a perfect father. Ideal, irreproachable.

It is a battle – against myself and against all the rest. I am at war with a formidable enemy. I hit my opponent, over and over, wearing myself out. And, every day, a new colossus stands before me for yet another unequal fight. He doesn't feel the force of my blows, the pain from the wounds I inflict. He never gets tired.

I struggle, and whenever I get a moment's peace I start to worry. I worry that I'm getting distracted, that the enemy is advancing on me, unseen. Every instant of happiness is a prelude to chaos.

This war is my inheritance, and I will pass it on in turn to my son. He who was born a second time with a burst of machine-gun fire.

I am at war against all those who try to think for me. At war against events. At war against fate. At war against life. At war. At war for him. At war against him too.

Sometimes I have the impression that a wall rises between us. He is on the other side. I see him pacing around. He can't hear me. He's in his own world. It's not that he's not listening to me, more that I'm not speaking to him. He's there, in his little goldfish bowl, and I am watching him from mine.

I need to reassure myself, to grant myself some victories, however hollow they may be. So, from morning until evening, I tick off the boxes of my to-do list.

Wake up on time. Hugs and kisses. Get dressed. Breakfast. Brush teeth. Go to day care. Come back from day care. Bath time. Dinner. Brush teeth. Hugs and kisses. Go to bed on time. Oops, one last pee. Back to bed.

To provide more structure, I also set up a marking system. Each day, I start with ten points. If I fail to accomplish a task, I lose a point.

If I do it, but do it badly, I lose half a point. When things get done but the expected result does not materialise, I lose a quarter-point.

So, in the morning, for example, if I make his toast and he eats it while sitting at the table, I keep all my ten points. If I don't have time to make his breakfast and we have to rush out the door and I forget his biscuits on the kitchen table, then I start my day on nine points.

If I've forgotten to buy bread the day before and all we have in the apartment is chocolate biscuits that would make a nutritionist choke on her kale, I lose half a point.

If I have made his toast but he's in a bad mood that morning or he's not hungry and we head out to the childcare centre with Melvil sulking and me gripping a fistful of toast, then I lose a quarter-point.

I don't try to understand what I'm doing. I just want a good mark. I want to be a five-star father. I want people to leave rave reviews about me on Dad. com: 'Wonderful! The best father in Paris!'; 'It is rare to find a father providing such a perfect education, but Antoine exceeds all expectations!'; 'Everything was delicious, from wake-up time till bedtime, particularly the generously foamy bath. A meticulously prepared week, with just the right amount of creativity.'

I arrive at the childcare centre on time: I keep all my points. I arrive there late: I lose a point. I arrive there at the last minute, carrying Melvil on my shoulders so I can get there faster: minus half a point. I arrive there late because he was dragging his feet: minus a quarter-point.

That first mark tends to set the tone for my day. From that moment on, I know whether I'm going to have to make up lost points, whether I'll be able to grant myself a few moments of weakness, whether I'll have to make sure I don't let anything get past me. When my homework is perfect, I sit in the front row; when I feel like being naughty, I sit at the back of the class.

I adapt this marking system to everything we do. For the bath: is it ready on time? Does he wash himself? How much water is in the tub and how much is on my shirt? Dinner: does it get eaten? A lot or just a bit? With or without vegetables? Etc. Everything is marked.

Sometimes, I manage to negotiate extra points, which I hoard and cherish like a child receiving pocket money for the first time. If we go to the swimming pool on Sunday, if he puts his coat on without help, if he does a beautiful drawing, if he learns a new word, if I get him to do his homework

just like the teacher asked him to, then I give myself
a point.

An extra point for when I don't have any left. A
token that I can put into the machine if I ever
run out.

In the show home of his life, Antoine obeys the
good father from those books on educating children.
Sometimes, the invisible authority makes comments
in addition to Antoine's marks. These comments are
often arbitrary and difficult to accept.

The comments, like those in a school report, are
judgements on Antoine's attitude, how much interest
he showed, how hard he tried. They recognise good
intentions, ethical dilemmas.

Was I generous enough with my attention when
I took Melvil to the park? Did I get bored while I
was pushing him on the swings? Did I read the story
with enough heart or did I rush through it so I could
have a glass of wine?

The comments are made in the evenings, when
I'm alone, at the moment when the weight of responsibility pins me to the sofa. I would like to leave
myself in peace, give myself a chance to live.

But I don't. I tally up my points and I listen to the comments.

I accept that I have been a five-out-of-ten father. That I must work harder. I promise myself I will try to do better tomorrow.

But when the comments are really bad, when the invisible authority says things like 'A disappointing day from Antoine; he must pull himself together' or 'Antoine seems to pay no attention to what is happening in class' or 'Antoine has potential but makes no effort to fulfil it' or 'Antoine spends more time watching rain pour down the windowpane than concentrating on his maths assignments' or 'Antoine's careless attitude is disturbing his son's development', then I seem to see a terrifying stranger looming in front of me, drowning me in its shadow.

It's that stranger telling me off in the street because I'm not old enough to smoke. It's that teacher warning me that I'm wasting my gifts. It's my grandmother catching me stealing money from her purse. That friend asking why I betrayed him. That lover asking why I'm so bad at loving.

It is all that shame and all that fear. When life tells you to take a good long look in the mirror.

When you can't tear your eyes away. When you look for your reflection and the mirror is empty.

I take Melvil to the park every weekend morning. Each time, we see the same lady. She is in her forties, with a wide face and small, round, dark eyes. She has a constellation of freckles covering nose and cheeks. There's a hint of childhood in her face, which is carried on into her long, curly brown hair.

She has pale skin and a marked elegance. She wears trousers, usually quite dark, with shirts that are white or sometimes blue-striped, and court shoes, which she wipes clean with a tissue when she sits down.

She stays for most of the morning, sitting on the bench at the other side of the playground. She reads her magazine religiously, from first page to last. She has no child here, not on the slide or the rope bridge or the climbing wall.

I have invented several lives for her before settling on one. I imagine that she's a lawyer or a radiologist – some highly paid profession, in any case, requiring years of higher education. She comes to the park every day to witness the beautiful aspects of childhood. The world of play, imaginary countries squeezed into this small space, a never-ending mad scramble, warm tears that the children's parents drink as if it were some magic elixir.

Then, just as my horizon is clouding with the sausages and mashed potatoes I have to make for lunch, the load of laundry I have to put in the washing machine, the colouring I have to supervise, she leaves – with the satisfaction of having other views to contemplate.

Some evenings, I wish I could disappear like she does. Just abandon everything. Let life take care of itself. Let some good, competent parents take control of the situation.

Several times, I have written this message for my sister: If anything happens to me, take care of Melvil as if he were your own son, as if I'd never existed.

I haven't sent the message. I haven't needed to. Not after that week when I thought I'd lost him.

That Monday, when I was picking him up from day care, they told me he wasn't feeling well. They said he'd spent all day in his corner and seemed to need rest.

I have lots of things to do, and the next day, when I wake up, I check his temperature and decide it's not too high: I can leave him with the women at the childcare centre. At the end of that day, they repeat what they'd said the day before, more emphatically this time. In the tone of their voices, I hear the beginning of a reproach: 'Melvil really isn't well.'

I act as if I don't hear this and wait until Thursday to keep him home. Three days when I pretend that everything's fine.

I wait until I have no choice, until the day-care ladies turn their advice into an order.

Orders must always be obeyed.

'Melvil must stay at home and get some rest. And you should take him to see the doctor.'

I swallow my saliva and submit to their command. I drag the pushchair backwards. He sits inside, silent.

I feel guilty. I relied on those women instead of relying on myself and now my son is ill.

Back at the apartment, his symptoms suddenly seem obvious. He won't eat a single thing. He starts crying when I try to put him to bed. He sulks on the sofa when I offer to play with him. He makes me pay for my thoughtlessness.

It takes the doctor less than a minute to make his diagnosis: bronchiolitis, an ear infection and teething pains. In the days that follow, Melvil's temperature continues to rise.

A young child with a fever is a body reconnected with its animal nature. A being that is fighting against itself.

The combat is internal and overpowering; he's not really there any more.

By Saturday, he's completely exhausted. The day is divided into half-hours. The first is for crying. Nothing is right, as far as he's concerned. He doesn't want to drink or eat or play.

He doesn't like music or stories any more. He doesn't want to go for a walk. The next half-hour is for sleeping. He collapses with fatigue, but his inner turbulence won't allow him more than a few minutes of rest.

For the past two days, he hasn't slept through the night. For the past two days, we haven't slept through the night. In the evening, I take him to my bed and we settle into his rhythm. We take short naps and, the rest of the time, we cry.

I doze off for a moment. Longer than a moment. A few hours later, I wake up with a start. I heard something. At last I open my eyes. He's not in the bed. A yell rings out, like someone who's been stabbed in the gut.

For a second, as the blade penetrates, I abandon myself to the pleasant sensation it brings: the cold metal in the burning flesh, the unknown piercing me, the infinite sinking through.

In the next second, I am suddenly aware of approaching death.

It's now. He fell out of bed. I am going to die. I jump up and hold him in my arms. Hug him tight. Undress him to make sure everything is still there.

I bend his joints one by one, making sure that he hasn't broken anything. I listen to his chest, palpate his little body, monitor his reactions, on the lookout for any signs of pain.

I build a wall of pillows to protect him. He presses himself against me. His face is streaming with sweat and tears. At his age, he still cries with his whole head: his face tenses, reddens, explodes in a shrill sound that comes out through his nose. Later, he will cry with his belly. That is the time of real sorrow, which can be shared and consoled.

I watch him as he slowly falls asleep.

The next day, when we wake, we are both surprised that we have slept for so long. As if his fall last night brought an end to his fever.

He gets up but keeps his arm close to his body. I think maybe it just hurts a bit. I try to make him move it. He growls at me. This time, I panic and take him straight to the accident and emergency department.

The doctor has the knowing look of a friend you've forgotten but who instantly recognises you. 'What happened?' he asks me. I'm surprised by his question. I wasn't expecting it and I don't know how to answer it. I should have told him: I'm a bad father and I let my son fall out of bed. An impossible confession, so I lie. I tell him we were playing together and he fell.

He orders some X-rays and a nurse takes us into the radiology room. She has rectangular glasses and her smile is sincere and unrestrained. She asks Melvil how he hurt himself. He growls again.

In this room, which looks like the control room of a Soviet-era nuclear power plant, she tells Melvil to stand straight. I find myself imitating him, frowning with concentration, perfectly still and silent. We are two criminals having our mugshots taken.

I plead guilty. Guilty of not doing anything, of doing it badly. I am given a suspended sentence: to be a single father. Condemned to be something I am not. I want to run away. I don't want them to catch us – just let us live our lives like this, like two escapees from the ordinary world.

They have caught us, photographed us, taken our names, filed us away ... and then our prison guard releases us.

After a while, the doctor returns, holding the X-ray, and tells me: 'He hurt his shoulder a bit, but there's nothing broken.'

I don't think I've ever been so relieved. I look through his body in the black-and-white image, turn to him and tell him the same thing Hélène told me a few years before: 'Even your skeleton is beautiful.'

We leave the hospital and the din of traffic surrounds us. The white light of this early-April morning spreads over the pavement. We are careful as we walk not to disturb it.

It's a perfect spring day. We decide to grab a chocolate éclair and go for a walk. He holds my hand.

Time to lay down my arms. Time to accept a life that I didn't choose. Acknowledge my defeat so I don't run away. Take off our shoes and have a foot hug. Laugh like madmen. The little monster wriggles as I tickle him.

I love the sound of his yelling. I know by heart the rhythm of his hiccups.

Time to be a child. To not be able to say who we were. To not know who we are. To understand that it doesn't matter. Hug him from behind. Breathe in his smell. Nibble his soft skin. Be a father.

4

December 2017

I decided that it was time. That Saturday, for lunch, I make him ravioli in a bolognese sauce and place his fork and spoon either side of his plate. I don't say anything, as if my words might ruin the moment.

To start with, he does it himself. He eats three mouthfuls while I watch, sitting on the other side of the table. Then suddenly he stops and points, signalling that it is now time for me to feed him.

'I'm not going to do that any more,' I tell him. He doesn't react, so I threaten him: 'If you don't eat it on your own, you'll have to take your nap without having lunch' – the kind of threat that parents never carry out.

Melvil picks up his spoon while giving me a determined look. Without taking his eyes off me, he plunges the spoon into his bowl, pulls out a ravioli, red sauce dripping from it. Then, looking pleased with himself, he drops it on the living-room floor. The sound the ravioli makes when it hits the wooden floorboards is the sound of a crushing defeat.

I am speechless. I stare at him, in shock.

There is always a moment of hesitation before the punishment. A moment when I try to work out what the appropriate response should be. It lasts a second, never longer than that.

He looked at me as he did it. That proves it was intentional. The time it took the ravioli to pass from the plate to the floor demonstrates premeditation. The look of satisfaction on his face constitutes an aggravating circumstance.

The punishment will be a forceful warning. I raise my voice. I tell him that, if he does that again, I will carry out my threat. I remind him that he knows me and that I will do it.

He does it again.

It takes me much less than a second this time. I slam his bowl against the table, in the process painting the ceiling red. My anger is cold and hot. I pick him up and put him in his bed.

When I close the door, I am still trembling with rage. He didn't dare utter a word. Alone in the living room, I am forced to accept my punishment.

In a panic, I send messages to all the mothers and future mothers I know, telling them what I've done.

At last, my sister replies. I tell her what happened, distorting the facts just enough to make my reaction appear justified. She says I did the right thing, even if it's not something she'd ever have dared do herself.

Melvil is paying for both of us. I try to calm myself down by walking quickly through the apartment. An hour later, unable to stand it any longer, I open his bedroom door. My son is sleeping, fists clenched.

I lean over his bed, take off his stained bib, and kiss him tenderly as though I haven't seen him for weeks.

When he wakes up, the storm is not completely over. We play together all afternoon. I don't feel whole with him. The guilt makes me awkward and clumsy.

His nanny arrives at nightfall. I kiss him as if I'm about to set off on a long journey. Then I leave, promising myself I will return in one piece.

I did everything I could to make sure they didn't know I'd be there. Every time I received an invitation from the theatrical troupe who were adapting *You Will Not Have My Hate* for the stage in Paris, I replied: 'Later'. I thought: 'Never'.

I had to find a bad reason to accept. So I wrote. Writing gives me lots of bad reasons to do all sorts of things.

I wrote the beginning of a story, just like I've done dozens of times over the past couple of decades. A beginning that would never have an end. A *once upon a time* with no *happily ever after*. A work that would, in any case, soon be destroyed.

It was the story of a man who told the story of his life in a book. There were two stories, in fact: the one about the writing of the book, and then the real one, about the events it described.

When the book was published, the author was offered money for the theatrical adaptation rights. It was the third story-within-a-story, the only one that really mattered; the truth is only ever revealed at the end. Actually, that was perhaps the reason – the fear of discovering this truth – that I never finished any of my previous stories.

My character accepted the offer. Unquestioningly, he let things happen. He watched his life play out onstage, more beautiful than it was, and bigger too. Enormous, in fact. He heard those words twisting the truth. He saw the actor speak them in a voice that wasn't his. He saw the spectators come to watch the spectacle of his life. He saw himself become a shopkeeper, selling off all his emotions and anecdotes, sticking a price tag to each event in his life.

When the show was over, he felt something sour in the back of his throat. Something uncontrollable. And yet, when they asked him if he'd enjoyed it, he said yes.

I imagined that man saying yes just to escape the situation. That man said yes so he wouldn't have to say anything else.

But that sour something kept growing inside him. And he ended up feeling angry at the actor who had played him. The man, he thought, who had stolen his life.

*

The beginning of my story ended there. I added a note, imagining what happened next: he followed the actor after a show, then did it again the next day. Every day, he followed him. He became completely obsessed by this actor. He wanted to take back what had been stolen from him.

His anger grew with each passing night. Until, one day, sometime later, he read in a newspaper that the actor was getting ready to play a new role: he was going to play Roberto Zucco in a new staging of the play of that name by Bernard-Marie Koltès. A new life to steal. A new skin to wear.

My character took this as an insult. The man who had stolen everything from him was now about to give it all back. But it was used now: a story already told, a second-hand life.

At the end of the final performance of his play, my character decided to kill the actor. He wanted the two of them to die at the same time onstage.

In the epilogue, he would write the story of these events from his prison cell and the book would, naturally, be a bestseller.

*

Of course, there were similarities. And yet I didn't feel any between that story and mine. I was completely blinded by the fiction that came from my hands and my head.

I imagined that it didn't belong to me, incapable as I was of perceiving that the proximity of those two characters – the actor and the writer – was a clue that they were the same, interchangeable character.

I couldn't see that they were one and the same person, split in two to give me no chance in this battle against myself. Yet I was their instrument as much as their victim. And my fiction was their battleground.

So I had to remain ignorant of all this. I was Antoine, a writer in search of material for a story that needed some authenticity.

To find that, to imagine what my character might feel, I had to attend the play.

I imagine myself remaining professional: I wear the mask of an author researching the subject he wants to write about. But not the real author. Not the author of *You Will Not Have My Hate*, which has been adapted into a play.

I ride the metro to the Théâtre du Rond-Point. The very place where my defeat is being staged. Where my life is being performed.

I stand leaning against the door of the train. Two stations pass before I notice the young woman hiding behind her black hair, sitting at the end of a row of four seats.

The carriage is only half full, yet she has chosen to sit there, as close to me as possible.

I don't know what long-lost animal instinct allows us to sense when someone has noticed our presence, even though they give no sign of having done so. It's like an invisible chemistry connecting you to them.

Or ... I don't know what madness leads us to feel that we are being spied on by strangers when they haven't even seen us.

The woman doesn't move. Her body gives no clue to her intentions; it is still. There is only the flicker of blue light on her face that makes her look absent.

She slides a fingertip across her phone screen and the shadows on her face change shape.

I lean slightly forward to see what it is, on her screen, that absorbs her so fully that she no longer seems to be there.

She is scrolling through photographs. A parade of faces giving perfunctory smiles, sulky pouts, expressions of feigned surprise.

For a moment, I admire the perseverance of these twenty-first-century court clerks who record every moment of their existence as if keeping the minutes of a trial. Then the parade slowly comes to a stop, like a wheel of fortune hesitating between riches and bankruptcy.

An image stares out: it's a photograph of me. Or is it? I don't know. Maybe it's just my panic, my anxiety, projected onto the screen.

I tense against the carriage door. Motionless. I wait for the train to stop at the next station. The young woman walks past without a backward glance and heads towards the glass doors that open with a carnival din.

In Kafka's story, 'On the Tram' – one of only a few that were published during his lifetime – a young woman saves the narrator from his anxiety when she steps into the tram where he stands.

It is because she enters, because he observes, because he describes every last detail of her appearance, down to the shadow in the whorl of her right ear, that he manages to escape his own strangeness as he stands there.

She leaves and my own anxiety returns. The door alarm sounds, followed by that soulless voice announcing 'Champs-Élysées Clemenceau' station and the pneumatic wheeze of the door's tired mechanism.

I watch her walk away, incapable of distinguishing reality from dream. Suddenly, I am full of doubts. Did she look me up on her phone? Or did I imagine it? Did that young woman really exist at all?

I try to seek her out, but I can't remember how she was dressed, if she was tall or short, slim or plump. My strangeness slaps me in the face.

She heads towards the end of the platform, without turning round. Fear of going mad. The doors close and I see a man with a coarse, red face. He is swallowing the contents of a can of beer as quickly as he can. It's one of those large cans, designed to get you drunk.

He has two others in a plastic bag that hangs below his knees. When he gets home, he'll be able to open one and tell himself that it's his first of the night.

An alcoholic's reflex. If you drink something without being seen, you didn't drink it.

Is all of this real? Did I actually live through that moment? Or am I creating a setting, characters, a story?

I remember that the train was moving slowly, that it slowed down again.

Franklin D. Roosevelt station. I head towards the door and the man staggers forward. He looks like a sailor, back on land after a long voyage.

I look at him without seeing him. He stares at me, like the young woman, like all the other occupants of the carriage will soon do, like those people waiting for me on the platform.

Suddenly I feel dizzy. They are all there to remind me – each in their own way, all of them in the same voice – that I have lied and betrayed.

I can act as if this character had been imprisoned in a book one day and that he will never come out.

But he is there, in this carriage, and everyone can see him.

And they all recognised him. I recognised him too. This father of words and paper imprisoned inside the 10,000 words that characterise him.

As long as the other's gaze is not fixed on me, I belong to myself, whole, flesh and blood, impenetrable. But whenever anyone looks at me, it's him they see.

I am like a glass prison. My prisoner imprisons me in a shamelessness that I despise. My wound, our wound, exposed to the eyes of the world.

And this father that I created, who is judging us. The ideal father, the other Antoine. I wish I could merge with him. Refer constantly to what he would do. What he would write. What kind of father he would be.

He is the one with all the courage and self-sacrifice, all the intelligence and serenity. He holds firm, while I collapse. I am the one with all the fear and anguish. I lurk in the shadows. He stands in the light.

At last the doors open. I am suffocating but I don't get out straight away. I hesitate for a second.

Why not just keep going? Why stop here? Why face up to this moment, when I could easily avoid it again?

I don't want to go there. I wasn't home, I didn't answer, I said maybe, and then one day he said yes and I was powerless to stop him.

So I get out because I have to. I need air. And as long as I can escape these lines that clasp me, these eyes that weigh on me, these characters that cost me, I will feel a little bit alive. Real. Tangible.

A woman on the platform is waiting for me to decide. I get out. As I walk past her, I think I hear her whisper: 'Hurry up, they're waiting for you!'

I turn round as the doors are closing. She smiles discreetly and then the train buries itself in the tunnel at the end of the platform.

Discreet smiles are the most precious kind. They are like gentle kisses, a hand on a shoulder, a delicate whisper, they are given without expectation of anything in return. For the space of a second, she reminded me of that taste that words will never have. The ascendancy that reality has over literature. The power of the ephemeral.

What's beautiful about a discreet smile is that it disappears immediately after appearing, without leaving you the words to describe it.

She told me: 'They're waiting for you.' She didn't talk about him. She didn't say: 'They're waiting for him.'

She said it with empathy, as if she could hear my pain, as if she wanted to soothe it, like a balm.

She said it with that intonation used by all the women I have loved in my life, the ones to whom I give all my defeats and who forgive me for what I am.

Very quickly, fiction captures me again. Its words scatter as my feet fall to pieces. I sink into the tarmac of the platform. Each step is a struggle. There is nothing to carry me now but my determination to escape.

Outside, at last, I can breathe all the air I want. It smells of Paris in winter: damp, grey, with a hint of ice.

Avenue Montaigne unfurls in all its golden sadness. The Théâtre du Rond-Point appears like a refuge for those who are lost.

Everything looks artificial, including this large Empire building, erected in honour of our armies and transformed into an avant-garde theatre by Jean-Louis Barrault's company.

When it reopened in March 1981, the first play performed there was *L'Amour de l'amour*, based on texts by Apuleius, La Fontaine and Molière. On the bill today, in the small hall, is *You Will Not Have My Hate*, with Raphaël Personnaz, based on the text by Antoine Leiris.

I find a place where no one can see me. Two large trees and a bush are growing outside the theatre and I hide behind them, like a child trying to escape punishment.

As a little boy, I often used to hide. In trees, behind bushes, under the bed. Not for any particular game, just because I liked that feeling of belonging only to myself, of knowing that nothing and nobody had any hold over me. I liked hearing my parents call out my name and not responding.

Then I had to come out of my hiding place, be a son, a student, a brother, and – later – an employee, a husband, a father. One day, they will hide me again in a box and nobody will call for me to come out.

I have continued hiding all my life. And each time, when I returned, I pretended that I'd never gone anywhere. Nobody was fooled, but the people close to me accepted this little act, this permanent to-and-fro. The others left my life.

I am the absent friend, brother, son. The one nobody can really depend on. The one from whom people distance themselves out of fear of becoming too attached.

So there I am, hidden behind two tree trunks, a bush and an electronic cigarette. The play will start in two minutes.

I suck in all the smoke I can before finally heading into the theatre. I enter like a steam engine, leaving nothing behind me but two white wreaths, smelling of apple and cherry.

At the far end of the vast foyer, I see the last few spectators entering the auditorium. A young man stands in front of the door, welcoming the late-comers. He wears a sort of brown apron and a sky-blue T-shirt, the uniform of the ushers at the Théâtre du Rond-Point. They are all young trainee actors.

I stare at him and advance in his direction without ever taking my eyes off him, like a model on a catwalk, chin raised, absent expression, hoping that I won't break a heel before I reach my destination.

My body tenses. Not completely, not all at once, but little by little, piece by piece. My shoulders stiffen first, then my arms, which are now swinging independently of my control, then my legs, which move forward independently of each other, all coordination lost.

Soon I am there. I look like one of those little plastic men that Melvil plays with. I can't bend my arms or legs. My fingerless hands are useless. My eyes are wide and my mouth is frozen in a half-moon smile. I stand in front of him.

I would like some kind of greeting. I've just run a marathon with a sack of bricks hanging from my shoulders and I don't get a medal? Not even a bravo? He could at least give me the chance to tell him about the journey I've taken to get here, so that he can know I didn't fall, that nobody saw me, that I managed to pass unnoticed. Invisible.

He just asks me for my ticket.

I stare blankly.

I don't have a ticket. This play is based on my book. I tell him simply, as if apologising: 'I'm

Antoine Leiris.' He doesn't say anything. He looks
at me and finally says, in the tone of voice a nurse
might use when asking a patient to eat his soup: 'Do
you have an invitation?' I mutter that he should ask
the press officer. 'Are you a journalist?'

He asks this in a louder voice. He's a policeman
now and I am a motorist being asked to move my
illegally parked car. I tell him no, I'm not a journalist.
Well, not any more. Seeing that the forceful approach
isn't working, that I still don't understand what he
wants of me, he settles on a more neutral tone. Like
a young teacher, at the start of the day, asking his
students to take out their notebooks, he says: 'I'll
ask him.'

He calls out to one of his colleagues and asks her
to fetch C. from the press department, who should
be somewhere nearby. She goes upstairs as my
dignity sinks down to my socks. Soon my dignity
will smell like feet.

I wait at the entrance to the auditorium, obliged
to clearly state the identity I had hoped to hide. I
wanted to be a simple spectator and now this tactless
usher is forcing me to be the author, the person
responsible for this whole ludicrous situation, naive
enough to believe that they would let me in, no

questions asked, without informing the people onstage that I have come to see the play, without buttonholing me afterwards to ask me what I thought.

I am a little boy of almost forty who has just lost a game of hide-and-seek.

From the top of the stairs, C. signals that it's fine. She looks embarrassed, as if to remind her colleague of the sign that I wear on my back: 'Grieving husband'. He glances at it as I pass him and seems to mumble something resembling an apology.

My sign, my dignity that smells like feet and I sit in the back row, next to the aisle, despite the repeated invitations of another usher who is determined that I should sit in the middle of the front row.

'You'll have the best seat in the house!'

I don't need the best seat in the house. I don't want to sit in the front row. I've seen this play before, you know.

I tell him: 'I'm fine here, thank you.'

The house lights fade to black. The stage lights up and it seems to me that, during this brief moment of darkness, something has changed inside the theatre. It's imperceptible at first. Just an impression. It's very dark and yet I can clearly tell that something is different. And then I realise. It's the seats. The spectators' seats are now turned towards the back of the room. I can see their faces. They are shadowed half-faces, eyes without pupils, vacant stares.

They are all facing me. Everyone in the audience is turned towards me. The show is taking place here, at the far end of the back row in the Jean-Tardieu Hall.

I know this is all coming from me. I know that nobody saw me, but all the same I feel like they're watching me, judging me, and I feel a sense of shame at letting them perform the spectacle of our life onstage.

When the actor pronounces his first words, I think I am the only one to hear them. I am a waxwork dummy, immobile in my seat. With all those eyes on me, I hold back my emotions. I show no anger, no desire, no disappointment. Perhaps there is nothing to see here, after all.

One by one, the spectators turn to face the stage. Now I'm just one face among many. I feel the first stirrings of curiosity. For this story, for the piano that marks out the passing days, for the stage lights that come on. I am a listening post. I am a watch-tower. The words keep being spoken and at last I become the spectator I wanted to be.

I am swept along by the silences. I weep at absence. I laugh at life. I dissolve into the emotion that seems to flood through the room.

I think the actor is doing a good job. I understand that he is not me. I don't recognise myself – it's probably the voice. There's a heaviness to my low notes that he doesn't have. He's younger, or perhaps he's just lived fewer lives. He's lighter than me. He makes the text speakable.

There are moments of grace. That anecdote, when the father is trying to cut his son's fingernails and he thinks he's cut off his finger. There are those people who accost him in the street, whose voices he doesn't hear. There are the little jars of food from the mothers of the other day-care kids. There is the letter that the father reads at the funeral. The puddle of water that father and son jump into as they leave the cemetery.

All of this resembles us but it's not us. I don't recognise that father. It's not mine or Melvil's. I am listening to someone else's story. I am hearing about someone else's son.

The writing has frozen us in a moment that no longer exists. I understand that this other father inside me, this ideal, is a fiction. The figure who was preventing me from being a father, who was making me feel dishonest, is merely a figment of my imagination. We are so different. I am going to be able to leave behind this burden. Let him have the demands of perfection. I will settle for roughly, almost, not quite. Let him have the shadow of artificial light. I will take the sun, the moon, the true.

The play gives this moment its movement, its flesh, the implacability of the present. And, in doing so, it frees us. We don't have to carry it any more.

The beautiful part is there, in the distance, treading heavily on the boards of the stage and making them creak. We have the rest. All the rest. The living part.

The stage fades to black. The house lights come on and I extract myself from the seat like someone

ANTOINE LEIRIS

struggling out of an unwanted embrace – and leaving a part of himself behind. Something will remain there, in the theatre. Perhaps the idea that I am the father of a book that is no longer mine.

The idea that I should act the way that father would act. Make the decisions he would make. Be the father that everybody admires and pities.

I open the door to the lobby like a man escaping his prison cell and it closes behind me on a story that is no longer mine. That father and that son are characters.

I think about Hélène. I gave her away and she had no say in it. I want to rediscover her, the way I've rediscovered myself.

I wish I could see her and tell her that she is, once again, just for me.

As I leave the theatre, I turn on my phone. A text from my sister: 'Hello Antoine. Since we'll be skiing at Christmas, I wanted to ask in advance if you had any ideas about a present for Melvil?'

I reply: 'A new papa.'

I think about him.

I can't wait to see him again and I can hear myself telling him: 'Who cares about the bolognese stains on the ceiling! From now on, you and I are going to play. I've found our life again. And it's an exclamation mark.'

5

January 2018

I took Melvil for a walk in the forest of my child-hood. I say 'forest' because I still remember how it seemed when I was young: a vast land of gigantic trees.

In reality, it's a wood, a small wood squeezed between three small towns in this middle-class suburb. The sort of wood where you could never get lost, with a playground in a clearing at its centre.

I want Melvil to feel this lightness around us. I want to gently lead us out of our comfort zone. To find new places, a new focus. Instinctively, I turn towards the places I knew as a child.

*

We are on the swings. He sits in my lap. I lean backwards until I am almost horizontal and he is lying on top of me. Our heads tilt back towards the sky.

Gravity is gradually inverted: as we move back and forth, we become a fixed point and the universe swings around us.

Further off, there's a wooden construction – a sort of Robinson Crusoe's cabin, but with chestnut trees instead of palm trees. We can hear a train rattling past at regular intervals, one of those old suburban trains.

You can climb to the top of this cabin using a rope ladder. The first few times, Melvil turns away from this obstacle, which is too big for someone his age. He doesn't like climbing or jumping or hanging, but he looks at that rope ladder with a mixture of fear and eagerness.

Melvil is not a fan of danger; it's not so much that he's afraid, he's just waiting until the level of expected enjoyment is high enough to justify the risk.

I follow him everywhere he goes, his shadow and protector.

We look after each other, like a pair of mountain climbers. Him above and me below. He looks back at me every time he edges up another inch.

Most of the adults sit on benches, but I'm right there, in the middle of the playground. I can't be like those other parents. I'm incapable of that kind of serenity.

I don't trust the vagaries of chance. Life has taught me that my slice of toast will always fall jam-side down. So there I am, watching over him, playing with him, and in the end I persuade myself that this is what Melvil wants, what he demands from me.

This time, we decide that the moment has come. We both feel the same way: better to get it over with, like quickly tearing off a sticking plaster or swallowing a spoonful of medicine. Like your first cigarette, your first kiss.

We close our eyes, empty our minds, and just do it, feeling certain that it's now or never.

He plucks up the courage, doesn't look down. And then, as if he's done it a hundred times before, he climbs the rope ladder.

I watch him from a little further away. I force myself not to stand just beneath him, guiding him, ready to catch him if he falls. I want this victory to be his.

He reaches the top and immediately starts worrying about how he'll get down. He calls for me and holds out his arms, as if he's drowning. I say: 'The easiest thing is to walk across the rope bridge and then go down that slide over there.' I point the way.

We negotiate – 'No, I want you to carry me … In your arms … I don't want the rope bridge.' I swallow the urge I feel to hold him in my arms, to wrap him up in cotton wool and put him away in a drawer so nothing can ever happen to him.

In the end, he agrees to keep going, and a minute later he lands, bottom-first, in the sand beneath the end of the slide. He smiles triumphantly, like someone who has overcome adversity, surmounted the insurmountable, passed the impassable, vanquished the invincible, all on his own.

He's not the first and he won't be the last, but that doesn't matter to me: he did it, he went all the way, he made it to the end. It is a victory, not only for him, but for me.

I let him take all the glory, but I am quietly satisfied with my role in this tour de force. I am the Sherpa, guiding the explorer to the summit. He could have hurt himself, but we'd both have survived.

There is an ambivalence at the heart of a parent's love. The defeats, scars and sorrows that children suffer help us to feel useful, like wolves licking their pups' wounds.

Should we expect them? Encourage them? Yearn for them? All the same, we hope that they are not too serious. Hence the ambiguity of this paternal love. He falls and I kiss him better. I become an orthopaedic surgeon.

At other times, I'm an ornithologist. I observe him as he sits down to eat. I don't move a muscle, I make no sound. I hold my breath for as long as possible, hoping that he won't notice my presence. I monitor every detail of his daily diet. I dissect his relationships with his peers. I study his song. I note the slightest change in his migratory cycle when he returns to perch on our branch every evening.

I am an oceanographer. I observe his adaptation to the aquatic environment. Sometimes he's a sailor, sometimes a whale, but always he's surrounded by small amphibious vehicles and little plastic fish.

I am a morphologist. As I dry him with a towel, I check that he's growing normally. That everything is in the right place and progressing on schedule. I am a bacteriologist. That little red spot on his left buttock worries me. I am a chemist. I ensure that he is receiving the correct dosage of vegetables to avoid any possible side effects.

I am a volcanologist. I can sense when the lava is heating up and predict precisely the date and time of the eruption. I study the lava flows after they've cooled to work out what elements they contain. I am a biologist. I observe how nature reasserts itself once the violence is over. I am a cartographer. I trace the borders of his life. I say where he can and can't go.

I am a hydrologist. I determine exactly when he must pay his last visit to the toilet, depending on the quantity of water consumed and the probability of leaks during the night. I am an astronomer. I calculate the duration of each of his revolutions and use this information to decide the time when he should wake up and go to bed. I am a historian. I tell stories, never forgetting to separate the facts from their interpretation.

I am a physicist. I work out, based on his weight–power ratio and the overall mass balance, when I should remove the stabilisers from his bike. I am a statistician. I predict the time and the number of attempts needed to achieve something. I am an anthropologist. I will note down for posterity his evolution when he finally starts acting like a big boy.

First, my childhood forest. Then our first apartment.

I have errands to run in this arrondissement. I hardly ever come back here, as if I erased this area from my map of Paris, which is now limited to the south and the centre.

I have to officially change my address for the electoral roll, so we go to the town hall in the eighteenth arrondissement. The square outside is lively. There's a merry-go-round and, at the back of the square, a large, empty church: Notre-Dame de Clignancourt.

On our way out, I suggest we go for a walk around the neighbouring streets, the way we used to when he was a baby.

We head back towards Montmartre. The place is so familiar, I can taste the memories.

Melvil is hungry; instinctively, we go to the Nord-Sud café, opposite the mayor's office, where we used to go every weekend to eat the home-made cooking that we never knew how to make ourselves.

He asks for spaghetti bolognese. I feel good. This place still contains what we left behind here: the pleasure of a shared moment.

His meal arrives. Melvil devours the pasta while I tell him about the first weeks of his life. I've never really done this before. The bedroom where we shoved two beds together to make one enormous bed; the family visits that we would cut short so we could spend time together, just the three of us; the mornings on the activity mat, watching in wonder every movement he made, the funny way he had of looking at us, of being there.

I remember our happy days, letting each memory develop while it's still hazy, taking the time to savour it and, as soon as it starts to become more precise, as its edges come into focus, as it grows more real and the mask of fantasy slips, closing that door and opening another one.

He isn't really listening. He eats huge mouthfuls of pasta. He can tell that I'm happy, that talking to him makes me happy. It's enough for him to eat everything on his plate. Well, apart from what he's spilled on the table, on the floor, all over his trousers and shirt and napkin.

Another day. It's almost summer. We're on a bus, on our way back from the zoo. In his cotton shorts, he jumps up at every stop and repeats – imitating the neutral feminine voice of the recorded announcement – the name of our next destination.

I see nothing, I hear nothing. After a morning spent walking, jumping, talking, scolding, laughing, wiping away chocolate stains, all that remains of my attention is for him. 'Olympiades', 'Choisy', 'Italie', 'Moulin-des-Prés' …

'Bobillot-Tolbiac'. I suddenly wake up. Before Melvil has time to understand or argue, I grab his hand and drag him to the rear door. I want him to see this place and I want to see it for myself again. Something remained there. It's a magical place, so magical that Hélène and I never went back, maybe out of fear that we would break its spell.

The doors close, leaving us under a May sun, outside 24 rue Charles-Fourier. A large building rises up before us, pink or perhaps almost purple.

I remember the early-evening sunlight skimming the surfaces of that bright June day. The music echoing through the streets. The phrases I kept repeating to myself before I arrived. Reminding myself to tell her that she's beautiful. To compliment her shoes. To ask her if she'd like to go for a walk and maybe have a drink.

I walk more quickly. He runs along the street beside me, hanging from my arm, until we reach a small, shady square. I recognise it instantly and relive that moment, just before, when nothing is sure yet, when anything could still happen. Move closer to her face. Put a hand on her warm, white cheek. Feel the skin of her neck under my fingertips, glimpse the corners of her mouth as they rise in a smile.

The traffic noise fades. People are sitting at tables on a terrace. Melvil follows me into the café. I ask a waitress if we can take a bowl of chocolate ice cream over there, to the middle of the square where there's a little grassy area with a playground.

He hasn't said a word since we got off the bus. Melvil is normally so chatty, but right now he's silent. We walk over to the low wall encircling the park. We sit next to each other. I hold the bowl while he excitedly digs his spoon into the ice cream. At last I kiss him.

I say: 'This is where your mum and I first met.' I had kept this memory in reserve for so long. My voice betrays something beyond his knowledge.

I say: 'This is where you were born.' Born from that love that I thought was behind me but that catches up to me now that we are here, the two of us, in the very place where Hélène and I once sat.

He asks: 'In Paris?'

'Yes, in Paris.'

I let the emotion come, the intimacy. I let it enter me again. I am not going to abandon it at the door any more or throw it in a skip. I will open the windows and lower the walls.

Another Sunday, we get in the car and drive wherever the road takes us. I am not really surprised when we end up in the neighbourhood where my grandmother lived, not far from the forest of my childhood and its swings. A housing estate like many others, with its clean streets and its children riding bicycles.

My grandfather bought a plot of land there in the sixties. My grandmother tells the rest of the story: he came back one day and without warning he announced that he'd found the place where we were going to live. They had their house built there.

I didn't show it to Melvil; only the streets, the 'path of madness' that I would ride down on my bike at top speed, and those other houses, each of them different but clearly marked by the style of their era.

There's that square house where the ground floor is half buried and the living rooms are on the first floor. Above the bay windows are striped awnings: white and yellow or white and blue.

And there's that other white building designed to look like a country farmhouse, with its fake thatch roof. And that artificial lake inhabited by a pair of white swans.

*

I park nearby and take Melvil out of his car seat. I suggest that we walk to the water's edge and throw his biscuit crumbs to the birds. They come towards us. Something in their gait reminds me of the contempt that swans always seemed to feel for me when I was a child. As if their beauty and elegance, their long slender necks and fallen angels' wings, gave them a sort of superiority.

I warn Melvil to be careful not to fall, then tell him how – when I wasn't much older than he is now – I fell into that lake as I was throwing crumbs to the swans.

I describe my father jumping into the water to fish me out as the birds started attacking me.

Melvil seems surprised. You, Papa ... you had a papa too?

I tell him about their pecking beaks, my panic, the feeling that I was drowning even though I could stand up, my feet sinking slowly into the mud.

He doesn't understand everything I'm saying. But, without looking at me, he moves away from the water and stops giving food to those animals that were once mean to me.

*

Our walk takes us close to the tennis court. It was there, behind the fence, that I smoked my first cigarettes. A gang of us got together there after I'd stolen a few from my grandmother's pack of red Rothmans.

We walk past a house. I recognise it: I was madly in love with the girl who lived there. One of those adolescent passions that leave traces only because they never become anything substantial.

She was a tall, thin girl, much taller than me. Every afternoon, we would walk home from school together. I have forgotten her name and, now I think about it, she probably wasn't all that pretty, just tall and blonde. But she liked me.

Her house is as well kept as ever. I can still feel the shyness I felt as a boy. She and I walked side by side together hundreds of times but I never dared try to kiss her. I was dogged by that character flaw for a long time. Even when I was older, I would often kiss girls by accident rather than because I'd made a conscious decision or taken the initiative. I preferred it when they made the first move. I couldn't act differently, anyway.

For a long time, I lacked that ability to choose for myself, to be decisive. Life just happened to me.

I was a secondary character. An employer told me that I had potential, so I worked hard. A friend told me that I was important, and I idolised him. Hélène informed me that I was going to be a father, and I cried.

We go back to the car and drive through the narrow streets. I don't think or worry about where we're going, I just let my feelings guide me.

We follow the same paths I used to take as a child and a teenager, on foot, on bicycles, on mopeds. These itineraries were haphazard, visual; I never knew where I was exactly or the names of any streets. I would just take the second turning on the left after the traffic lights on the corner with the newsagent's; the road on the right of the hairpin bend after the stop sign, etc.

So we take the second street on the right after the old Prisunic supermarket, left at the church, and then the next right, at the sign for the Topy shoe repair shop.

My old school is located halfway down a steep slope. It consists of two large buildings that I instinctively associate with the nineteenth century

and the Third Republic, although I don't know
enough about architecture to be sure about that.

The bigger kids – from Year 4 to Year 6 – were
in the upper building, which used to be the boys'
school. The younger kids – Year 2 and Year 3 – were
in the lower building, which used to be the girls'
school. A staircase links the two, so everyone can
go to the cafeteria.

I park the car. We get out and walk towards the
buildings. I think about the Frank Capra film, *It's a
Wonderful Life*. James Stewart attempts suicide on
Christmas Eve, believing that his life is a failure,
but an angel – a beginner who hasn't earned his
wings yet – manages to save him. In order to
convince him to keep living, the angel takes him to
all the places that marked his life, showing him how
things would be if he'd never existed.

I think: I am making that same journey, guided
by the little angel who is holding my hand.

Outside the buildings, I tell Melvil how, at more
or less the age he is now, I used to come here every
day of the week, that this was my school. I point
out the headmaster's office and the school nurse's

room, and I realise that part of myself was made there. An insignificant moment that, nevertheless, changed me quite profoundly.

In our class, as in every class everywhere, throughout history, there was one really big kid. The boy who towered over the rest of our class was called Patrick. He was practically a man, with frizzy hair and a voice that had already broken. He wasn't a nasty kid, and he rarely used his strength, but he was still intimidating. He intimidated me.

On the day we were supposed to get vaccinated, we were standing in line in the playground and I saw Patrick suddenly appear, in tears. The headmaster was dragging him forward and Patrick was yelling: he didn't want to get an injection. This massive, powerful boy was exposing his panic to the eyes of us all.

I remember feeling a shiver run through the entire line of children. As if that possibility – of refusing, saying no, fighting against something, which had never even crossed our minds before – had awakened the dormant anxiety within each of us.

Melvil is a newborn, only a few hours old. A nurse enters the room where Hélène and I are with

our son and tells us: 'We have to take some blood.'
She explains that it can be a hard thing for parents
to witness because they have to find a vein in the
baby's hand, which is often quite difficult.

She tells us that it would be better if we didn't
go with him, that he's going to cry a lot. I say that
if he can bear it, then so can I.

I am ten years old. I am standing in line. I go
into the nurse's room. My body tenses, my jaw
clenches. She gives me a shot and I don't cry.

I was one of the few who didn't cry that day.
From that moment, I drew a definition of my
strength. I wouldn't be the bravest person I knew,
or the most handsome. I wouldn't be the funniest
or the most intelligent. I wouldn't be the best
at sport or with girls.

I would be the one who stood up to pain the best.
The one who never let anyone see how much he
was suffering. The one who remains standing. That
little boy is still inside me.

I would like to take Melvil into the school, but
the walls are too high and the gate is locked on

Sundays. So I lead him down the slope, to find out whether we can see anything through the entrance to the music room.

On our way there, I see the place where we used to play marbles. It's not the same as it was. Our matches were played on a manhole cover, for keepsies. I remember that I never played with my best marbles because I was too afraid of losing them.

Instead, I would try to win the others' best marbles by staking several of my lesser ones. I didn't care about how many I had – I have never cared about numbers. I wanted the most beautiful ones, the most precious.

We cross the street to reach the highest point of this multilayered playground. I remember some large, barred windows in a sort of covered yard at the big kids' school, and I would like to see all that again.

Melvil doesn't really understand what we're doing here or what we're looking for, but he imitates me when I shade my face with my hands to check that nothing's happening in there.

Like him, I am four years old. We are the same height. Together, we stand and stare, with the same sense of yearning, at the school playground where we will soon grow and change.

There are ping-pong tables in the covered yard. Ours were wooden; these new ones are concrete. I used to graze my ribs, running around them. In my last year at the school, we would always take the table at the back. Nobody contested our right to that table because we were the oldest kids in the school.

Whenever I played competitively, I showed the same determination I had shown when getting my injection. I never gave up. I would pretend to be a good loser because I couldn't stand the humiliation of defeat. I always said I wasn't competitive, but as soon as I knew I couldn't win at something, I would instantly stop playing it. Later, I avoided all sports to spare myself this kind of unpleasantness.

I have a set of photo-booth snapshots from that era, when you could still move between each shot. Of course there are only three photos left out of the initial four, because the last one had been used for a travel card.

In each picture, I have the same petrified smile, the same contorted pose, the same absent gaze. I am gradually leaning closer and closer towards the part of the booth where the photographs would emerge. Perhaps, in the last image, I am simply not there at all any more.

There is sometimes a single, frozen image of ourselves that remains from our childhood. An echo of who we were, at that moment, in that place, with that attitude. For me, the image in my mind is of that evasiveness, that constant drift towards the edge of the frame, the idea that – if I don't make too much noise – nobody will notice that I am no longer in the picture. That I am invisible.

'Papa enjoyed some great victories here,' I tell Melvil. I describe the frantic scrambles, the skidding slides, the drop shots and smash shots.

These sorts of memories are not part of the story I have made of my life. As if they have remained in the places where they happened. Elsewhere, they are forgotten. They exist only here, and come to life only when I return.

*

Melvil is stunned at the idea that I could have done all these things. He stares at me in silence, baffled by why I have suddenly grown shorter, why we now seem to look so alike: the same boyish face, the same rabbit teeth, the same love of observing, the same mix of apprehension and determination, the same presence.

I can tell from the way he's looking at me that he can't imagine me anywhere else but in my armchair, doing anything but listening to the radio or cooking pasta shells — I have cooked dozens of kilos of pasta shells — or vacuuming the apartment. He can't imagine me falling instead of just helping him up when he falls. He can't imagine me yelling unless it's to tell him off. He can't imagine me not paying attention, crossing the street without looking, crying when I'm in pain.

I was the same. I could never imagine my father without a cigarette in his mouth, sitting behind the wheel of a car.

It's astonishing for both of us. I look at myself through him. I had forgotten the little boy that I was, just as Melvil can't imagine what an adult like me, with my tall, straight-backed body and my deep voice and my ironed shirts, would be doing in a school playground.

As if I'd always been the way I am now. As if I hadn't been a child myself. As if I couldn't be anything other than what I am: his father.

6

March 2018

For a long time, I wouldn't allow any screens at home. But I finally agreed that we could watch a film together every weekend.

I remembered one particular cartoon that I'd written about a few years before and that had fascinated me with its subtle, evocative power to offer the viewer various paths rather than imposing a straight narrative line. There were no good guys or bad guys in this film and the music was enchanting.

So, that Saturday morning, while we are still in our pyjamas, I suggest we watch *Ernest & Celestine* together while eating chocolate cake for breakfast. I want to have fun with him, to enjoy the story of this bear and this mouse, two species who are not supposed to speak to each other.

The bears above and the mice below.

I turn on the computer. For me, there are two shows at the same time: I watch the film and I watch Melvil, his eyes wide as he is thrilled by the sight of moving pictures for more or less the first time in his life. His initial smile of delight is gradually transformed into an irresistible frown of concentration.

I watch him watch. He is not even aware that I'm observing him, so absorbed is he by the song of the hungry bear and the little mouse who stubbornly refuses to follow the path laid out for her.

I listen to him eat. It's like an orchestra when he eats. Meat makes a sharp, clear sound, his teeth snap-snap-snapping. Rice and pasta are slower and more rhythmic as he chews big mouthfuls of them. A chocolate éclair is swallowed very quietly and ends on a sustained note of satisfaction.

Melvil jumps slightly when the bear sneezes, then puts his hand on mine when Celestine gets told off. He tenses like a bow during a frenzied pursuit through the sewers of the city, which have been colonised by the mice. His favourite cuddly toy, Doudou, gets an enormous hug when Celestine is finally reunited with Ernest.

At the end of the film, he turns to me and asks me to play out a scene that he especially liked. 'You're Ernest and I'm Celestine!' he says commandingly. He begins: 'But, Ernest ...' In this part, the bear and the mouse have just escaped from the police and are outside the bear's house. The bear then tells the mouse that she should go back to her own home while he goes to his. To which she replies: 'But, Ernest ...'

I speak my lines in a bear's voice – 'Sorry, no mice in the house!' – and walk away, before slamming the door behind me. He starts laughing and jumps off the sofa. 'But, Ernest ...' he says, with just the right amount of pleading in his voice.

He asks me to grab the collar of his pyjama top just like the bear does with the mouse before throwing him out of the house. 'NO MICE INSIDE THE HOUSE, EVER! You let one in, you get a thousand. That's what you all are like. Just ask any bear.' I throw him onto the sofa as he laughs uncontrollably.

'But, Ernest ...' His memories become more blurred; he starts getting words and episodes mixed up in his mind. He talks vaguely about a broom to sweep away mice, then mousetraps, and lastly glue traps, which Celestine says make the poor trapped mouse's heart explode.

'Is that what you want, Ernest? For my heart to explode?' I frown like a grumpy old bear. He says: 'Bears above and mice below? Is that it?' with the same anger as the real Celestine. Then he says: 'And you better stay upstairs, Ernest!' and – like the little mouse in the film – he pretends to head down to the cellar.

I don't remember the next line. Noticing this, he frowns reproachfully and says: 'You say ... And you stay downstairs, Celestine!' I obey and he plays the rest of the scene alone, miming the part of the mouse as she builds a makeshift hammock in the cellar.

We spend a whole day bathed in the purest form of happiness. For a few hours, I am no longer just Melvil's father, the one who gives orders, who lays down the law, the one who decides.

I am no longer just the one who draws the borders between good and bad, the alpha and omega, the beginning and the end, the judge and the cop, the priest and the Bible, the arbitrary and the just.

I am seven years old and I am spending my afternoon in the garden, hunting the spiders that hide under stones. I can clearly hear my mother calling me in for dinner.

I remember laughing hysterically with my sister, being secretly in love with her friends, spending whole Saturdays playing video games with my little brother without ever letting him win.

I remember being with friends, getting into trouble. I remember us climbing to the top of a tree and my friend Guillaume getting stuck up there. He cried until my father came to rescue him.

I rode my bike and I took hot, foamy baths, soaking in the water until my fingers were rough and wrinkly. I left my dirty clothes lying around my bedroom floor, I smoked my first cigarette, I loved my parents.

As I am putting Melvil to bed that evening, I am bombarded with memories of the smell of lilacs in the spring, the feel of chestnut burrs against my fingers in the autumn, the taste of sole fillets cooked in butter at my grandmother's house, the sound of my slippers hissing on the tiles.

Going into a skid on my BMX, making rainbows with a hosepipe, smacking a velvet armchair to send stars of dust flying through the sunlight, spitting out cherry stones like a cowboy, being hypnotised by the music of a ping-pong rally, hearing Keith Richards play guitar for the first time, seeing the road unfurling to the sound of David Bowie's voice in David Lynch's *Lost Highway*, emptying every drawer in my bedroom then tidying everything up again, learning to whistle, opening the window in the middle of winter to feel how warm it is under my duvet, running across the floor like a madman when it gets so cold I have to close it again, hearing my father complain about the wasted electricity.

And then this image: when I was young, our house was surrounded by immense-seeming walls. I couldn't say exactly how high they were, but my father could touch the top if he raised his arms above his head. He was five foot nine, so those walls were perhaps seven or eight feet high.

There was a pile of logs by the wall next to the garage, which made it possible to climb on top of it. For a long time, I was afraid to try. Then, one day, I followed my sister when she did it. Nothing ever seemed to scare her.

The first sensation, up at the top of that wall, was of danger, vertigo. But that quickly faded and became something else. An idea of pure, absolute freedom, of being subject to no laws other than the physical ones: if I put my foot there, I'll fall.

Up on that wall, I was nowhere. Not at home, and not at the neighbours' house, but in between the two.

That is another image of myself that I keep in my mind. Sitting on my wall, at the border: no nationality, no attachments, in international waters.

The next day, the trees are half bare, curled in on themselves, shivering with cold. The grass verges are dusted with white. The earth is hard, and so is the air.

The cold strips away all odours, leaving only the smells of stone and tree bark. In the dampness, a mist rises, transforming each street into a cul-de-sac.

I always loved those cold, damp mornings. It's still dark when we close the front door behind us. We can't see much, so we navigate by hearing. The sound of footsteps on frozen grass marks our tempo and shows us the way.

We exhale vapour and pretend to be smoking cigarettes. We're wrapped up in layers of coats and scarves. We enter the car like thieves.

We have to let the engine warm up. We rub our hands together and breathe on them. The air smells of petrol and hot plastic. My father wipes condensation from the windscreen with the back of his hand.

Melvil is in the back seat. His woolly hat is pulled down over his forehead and, in his red scarf, he looks like a Christmas elf. This isn't a special occasion, though, just another Saturday; we're going for a ride.

The car purrs along the perfect little streets. Surfaces shine with frost. There's nobody around, only ever taller gates and cars parked outside them. When we visit my suburb, it's easy to believe that the only inhabitants are automobiles.

I savour the beauty of the buildings, the presence of nature, the peacefulness. The gardens are neat, the streets clean; there's nothing out of place here. For a moment, I think we could come back here to live. But, very quickly, I remember the loneliness, the vacuousness, the feeling of being trapped.

I grew up in paradise, in the biblical sense of the term: a world of absolute peace that nothing could disturb. It was a painting, picture-perfect, but behind the scenes the brush strokes cut like scythes.

As a child, I cursed that place. You grow up within yourself when you grow up there. My parents died within themselves, as if trapped inside.

I park the car a few feet away. I unfasten Melvil's seat belt. I pull his hat down over his head again. He asks no questions; he is content to follow me.

It's icy cold. The two of us stand, now, outside the gate of my childhood home.

Back then, I thought it was enormous. There were three floors and a basement – so many hiding places. Today, it doesn't seem any bigger than the other houses.

My sister and I shared a room at the top of the house, in what used to be the attic. Two skylights in the roof. The carpet was electric blue and had a slightly rancid smell, a mix of dust and damp. Each of us had a little wardrobe of our own. Mine was full of cheap sweaters and navy-blue corduroy trousers.

My Sunday best was hung ready on a coat hanger. A white polo shirt that I used to button up to the collar, a sky-blue Velcro bow tie, and a pair of trousers with opal-green braces that had drawings of horse riders on them.

My parents' room was on the floor below. My brother was in the room next to theirs. When we were in the attic, in our bedrooms, we were always listening out for what might be happening below.

In that house, everything happened through noises, sounds. The dinner we could hear sizzling, the front door creaking open, the bath water running, and my parents.

Like radio listeners, we followed avidly as family life was put together and, later, as it fell apart.

My father had bought the house when it was a ruin so he could do it up. It was his life's work. He did some of the renovation himself. He restored the entire facade and fixed the roof. He smashed down walls to create a large, open space on the ground floor and he completely remade the first floor. He converted the attic into a bedroom for my sister and me.

I describe that building work to Melvil the way I experienced it at his age.

The constant hammering and sawing, the tools left lying on the floor which I would use for my games, my father's polo shirts stained with paint, his strength.

As if time had stopped, the house tells the story that we wrote almost thirty years earlier.

On the ground floor, there was the living room/ dining room and the kitchen. My father laid earth-coloured tiles on the floor there because it was cleaner and required less maintenance than floor-boards. The kitchen was too small and the wallpaper didn't match.

My father wanted to be the master of his house. He imagined himself as its patriarch, its creator, the builder of a home. But he never finished. Not the house or anything else. To finish something is to let yourself be judged on the results. He imagined that he had talent, but he never dared expose that talent to the cold air of reality. He preferred to depict himself as a misunderstood genius rather than a failed artist.

He wasn't just an accountant. He didn't bankrupt the company that he tried to start. He didn't leave his house a building site. Instead of facing up to and questioning this inability to finish anything, he blamed the outside world, other people, bad luck.

This finger-pointing distracted him from his own powerlessness.

'They' had underestimated the amount of work. 'They' had prevented him completing it. 'They' hadn't helped. This 'they' enabled him to avoid accepting his own limitations.

As I grew up, I created myself in opposition to this anger, this bitterness.

When he was very young, my brother used to throw up all the time, a constant torrent of vomit. In the end, my parents gave him water and fruit syrup in his baby bottle instead of formula.

Every time my brother was sick, it was my father who cleaned up the mess. The rest of us just looked disgusted. My sister started retching, while my mother said she couldn't stand the smell and locked herself in her bedroom. But my father cleaned up the puke without showing the slightest sign of repulsion.

So, despite his inability to complete any of his projects, I admired his day-to-day diligence. His role as father protected him from the stink of vomit.

In the same way, he never seemed tired. It was always my father who came to comfort us when we woke up in the middle of the night. It was my father who took us to our activities on weekends. He was immune to boredom and bad smells, to cold and heat.

My father was always there, in close-up. My mother existed in a permanent backwards tracking shot. She seemed to move away whenever we approached her. Her absence made my father indispensable. Her fragility made him tough. Her volatility made him stable.

So, while it was true that the kitchen wasn't perfect and there wasn't enough gravel to cover the driveway and his company had completely collapsed, at least he was always there for us. A father and his three children.

A while ago, Melvil threw up for the first time. Not just the usual baby spit-up, but the real thing.

A torrent of beetroot, pasta shells, sausage and banana. I had been looking forward to that moment.

He stared up at me sorrowfully and I told him: it's okay, no big deal, I'll clean it up. I went to fetch a hot sponge and some kitchen roll with the pride of a man who is finally about to enter battle.

I felt no disgust, no doubt, no discomfort. I cleaned it all up, I took the rug out of his room, I changed his clothes, I kissed him, and I felt strong.

For a long time, I cherished that part of my father. I admired him, I wanted to be like him. I thought he was handsome, with his fine dark hair, his high cheekbones, his gaunt cheeks, his strong chin, the shadows that covered his eyes whenever he frowned. He had a sailor's face.

I also remember his broad shoulders, his thick hands, his chewed fingernails. His thumbnails were yellow and misshapen. His index and middle fingers were brown from the cigarettes that he chain-smoked. He held them just above the filter and never smoked more than half of each. No sooner had he stubbed out the last one than he was lighting another.

In all the photographs of him in his youth, there's a cigarette between his lips. There he is, in tight jeans and fitted polo shirts. Always moving. Smiling.

When I started smoking, I used to steal his fag ends from ashtrays. I smoked his leftover Dunhill Internationals.

I don't remember many smells from my childhood, other than cigarette smoke. I couldn't stand that smell; for a long time, I told myself that I only started smoking so I wouldn't have to smell my father's cigarettes any more.

Only in one place was that smell transformed. There, its nature was changed. It was no longer a source of disgust, but the scent of freedom, an escape from the boredom and banality of everyday life. On Saturday mornings, a new world opened up. My sister, my father and I would walk to school – because in France we always had school on Saturdays – and we would stop at a café to buy a pack of cigarettes.

We go inside. The green and grey tiles whisper under our shoes. In those years, the most famous pornographic magazine in France is *Union*. Its front page is visible on the stalls in the tobacconist's. Back then, bare breasts are still a common sight on television and the vibrators on sale in La Redoute are presented as facial stimulators.

This is just before the rise of plastic surgery. Pamela Anderson would be the apogee and the end. Masturbatory, low-cut beauty.

There are croissants on the bar, but I always ask for toast. The taste of the butter slathered over the hot, crisp bread. My father smokes a cigarette.

The smell of his cigarette smoke mixes perfectly with the smell of my sister's hot chocolate.

I take Melvil into a bistro that does its best to recreate my memories of that long-lost café. I play the role of my father. I drink coffee and smoke cigarettes.

Outside the house, I see myself running down the driveway to open the garden gates so that my father can get the car out and drive us to school. I have to keep hold of the dog so it doesn't escape.

I remember that car; each object radiates memories, like a woollen scarf unravelling. Our car was not like anyone else's. Or rather, it was exactly like all the others: a Peugeot 505, a hefty rectangle of steel with yellow headlights and creaking doors.

It was its colour that made it different from all the others: it was copper, or a sort of lazy orange that faded over the years. Only a few metallic glints recalled its lustrous past.

When my father brought that car home, I could see the pride in his face. It was a saloon, the largest Peugeot on the market. He'd got a special deal on it. Nobody had wanted a car in that colour, and it had spent too long in one of those gigantic car parks in the Paris suburbs where new vehicles are lined up like ears of steel corn; in the winter of 1989, acid rain had eaten into the bodywork.

The rust went quite well with the original colour. It made the car look like the ginger boy in Jules Renard's novel *Poil de Carotte*. In the neighbourhood where we lived, I don't think anyone noticed that we possessed the flagship Peugeot. But everyone saw that our car was orange with freckles of rust.

As if to prove that he had really wanted that car, that he hadn't bought it just because it was going cheap, my father spent the rest of his life buying cars in unlikely colours. The next one was a drab olive green; another was plum blue; the last one, a faded burgundy. This was my father's only whim.

My mother didn't drive it. The Peugeot had no power steering and you needed rugby player's arms to manoeuvre it.

She tried driving it once, and Poil de Carotte ended up in a scrapyard.

My sister and I are at home that afternoon, I think, playing together. It must be a Wednesday, or the holidays. My father is at work and my mother is in bed.

After a while, she gets up and we hear her staggering towards the car. My father has borrowed hers that day – because there wasn't enough petrol in the Peugeot to get him to the office. We hear the door creak and slam shut. Without saying anything, she leaves us there with nobody to look after us and the feeling that we should expect the worst.

I remember it as though it had remained locked up in there forever, behind those high walls. That childhood waiting, breathing in the dread-soaked air, speaking the language of make-believe.

*

I was paralysed by fear. I felt like I was outside my own body. From above, I watched myself acting as if nothing was wrong. I was split in two.

I thought that fear would never leave me, that it was impossible to live without it. Then I became an adult and it is only recently that that feeling has returned. When Hélène died, I did everything I could to make sure Melvil never felt that fear.

A few hours later, or maybe just a few minutes, my grandmother came to fetch us. My mother had been involved in an accident. It had happened very close by, at the end of our street. The bend was more than a ninety-degree angle and she hadn't managed to turn the steering wheel quickly enough.

She had crashed into a tree, the first one on the opposite pavement, barely a hundred metres from our house. She hadn't been wearing a seat belt. Her forehead was wounded and she would bear the scar for the rest of her life.

My mother looked like her era. When she was feeling well, she resembled Marlène Jobert in a *Paris Match* photospread. She became that Julien Clerc song: 'Suffering at Your Hands Isn't Suffering'.

A discreet beauty, a vague sadness, the breath of life carrying you along despite everything. The impression of something going by too quickly.

That era is now over. Along with that scrawl in the middle of her forehead. Like a piece of earth, grounding my mother's twin poles – she was bipolar.

Those two continents with their contrasting geography, two tectonic plates that collided and shook our little planet.

When she wasn't feeling well, my mother transformed into that William Sheller song, 'Mama is Crazy'. There is nothing we can do. We are weighed down by the idea of a lost happiness, a melancholy hidden behind words, a melody to which we cling in order not to hear the rest.

I look at the tree. It's fine. No trace remains of the crash, and my mother has since died.

But it was that day, after the accident, that we realised there was not going to be a happy ending.

Melvil holds my hand. He wants to take Papa home.

7

July 2018

I go over to the bed. He is already awake. I ask him if he slept well. He tells me 'no'. He's covered in sweat and his eyes are vacant, as if he doesn't know who I am.

Did you have bad dreams? 'No.' Do you want to get up? 'No.' And no sooner has he said that than he falls into my arms, pressing his nose against my neck. His head is still damp, he smells of night. He smells of garlic too. Probably the cream cheese with herbs that he devoured yesterday on several slices of toast.

I love the way he smells in the morning. It's the smell of the present. The scent of the new day rising.

Something starting again at zero. It's sweet, hot and garlicky. Every day, I smell it; I go around sniffing the air, deliberately. As if to sniff out the idea that I, too, am allowed to have a day that is not just the one before or after another. In the mornings, I don't smell of a fresh start – just doubt, sleeplessness and cigarettes.

Do you want to go to the toilet? 'No.' With each successive no, I realise that this is not going to be an easy day. Sometimes children are like that. Parents too. Some days, I tell him off for no real reason, just to vent something inside me, simply because I need that confrontation. To feel that he's against me and then to press him against me.

How can you love something that you've never hated? I tell myself that he does the same thing.

Chocolate croissants? Bread and jam? A glass of water? Go for a walk? Play with your cars? Do some drawing? 'No', 'no', 'no', 'no', 'no' and 'no' again. He's testing me. He wants me to lose it. I stay calm.

The morning continues. His negative answers are accompanied by gestures. He stamps his foot. He throws his toy car. I tell him 'no' too. This is what he wants. He keeps acting up. This isn't a game. It's something else. Something more violent.

Once lunch is over – he says 'no' to pasta shells in butter, then swallows them without chewing – it's time for his nap. I am already tired. I tell myself the rest will do him good. That when he wakes up again, it'll be like a new morning. A morning where he'll want to say yes.

But he's restless, he can't sleep. He hasn't taken a nap since the start of our stay. This is the fifth day of the holiday.

The fifth day is pointless. This is not an observation or a theory, it's a universal law. If you go for a ten-day family holiday to any tourist destination, everyone always wants to be home on the fifth day. It's an indisputable fact.

The first day is arrival and discovery – you're busy. Then comes the time when you get used to things: you drink coffee, you eat chocolate croissants. After the fifth day, you can reassure yourself by thinking that you're more than halfway through. That you'll be going home in only another four days.

Melvil keeps calling me from upstairs. I don't think he's going to sleep. At 2 p.m., I decide we may as well go out. The beach isn't far away.

The bay looks magnificent under a white sky. Waves crash against the cliffs of Saint-Valery-sur-Somme. From the garden at the top, we get only a few splatters.

Hélène's mother and sister, and her sister's children, are with us. Everyone agrees we should go to the beach. The children think they've spotted some seals and they want to take a closer look.

I go upstairs to fetch him.

Do you want to come for a walk? 'No.'

We reach the top of the long flight of steps that goes down to the beach. The wind is blowing. We're wearing jackets. It's a steep descent.

As soon as I touch the first step, I feel a force at my back, pushing me. I have an urge to hurtle down the steps two at a time. I want to feel drunk on speed, let the lightness sweep me away.

Melvil holds my hand.

Race you?

'Yes!'

The first smile of the day.

*

He laughs like a baby – one of those laughs that explodes from the throat, like a hiccup. He squeezes my hand as hard as he can, but I can't feel his weight. He has no body any more. He is no longer too small, too shy or too sensitive. He is nothing but speed.

Abruptly, we find ourselves at the bottom of the steps. Looking up, the distance we've covered seems immense. It resembles a mountain road with hairpin bends. I half expect to see Tour de France riders cycling along it.

Melvil immediately wants to go back up so he can do it all again. Obviously, this is not going to happen. As I write 'obviously', I realise that words like that have no meaning.

Why 'obviously'? Because going for a walk means moving from point A to point B then moving back from point B to point A? Because it makes no sense to go up and down a flight of steps as many times as you need to feel you've had enough?

I don't want to walk on the beach any more than he does. I want to go back up those steps and come hurtling down them again just as much as he does. And yet we must join the others.

Because they're expecting us? Because we're there to go for a walk? Because we have to make the most of being at the beach? I don't know, but I raise my voice and he submits.

I have brought the bucket, spade and fork.
'No.'
The ball.
'No.'
Then go and play on your own.

I run off to play beach tennis. The wind cuts short our game. I can see him in the distance getting upset and his grandmother trying to calm him down. I walk over. Raise my voice again. Louder this time.

His face turns red. He starts crying. He rushes towards the sea. I grab his arm. He escapes. Stamps his foot. The wind blows harder. It gives us no respite; it sweeps away all sounds.

I am mute. He is deaf.

I grab him and hold him imprisoned in my arms. I feel the anger growing. I hear it thrashing around inside me. It barks at me the words that I will yell at him, even louder, to make him shut up.

He is crying.

I carry him up the steps from the beach, two at a time. It seems to take a long time.

The anger is still yelling at me. You must not do that. You are a bad boy. It's all I can hear. I can hardly breathe.

The wind crashes against the cliff. Up there, we feel only small gusts. I think he can hear the anger too. Or at least an echo of it.

He is starting to get scared. So am I.

Inside the house, I carry him straight to his bedroom. I put him down, feet on the floorboards.

'Stay here and tell me when you've calmed down!'

I slam the door. Sit on the floor with my back leaning against it. The anger falls silent. No, that's not true: the anger isn't silent. I can still hear it, only muffled now. It's inside the room, with Melvil, on the other side of the door.

How can I leave a child locked up with a monster like that?

I have the impression that that rage doesn't belong to me. I try to get rid of it. I wonder where it comes from. And I see my father again, behind the shutters.

I feel his anger again, as if he gave it to me that day. I experience it as a curse.

It's a few days after my mother's accident. We're in her car. He comes to a halt outside a brick building. She is sitting on her bed. Her bags are packed. All three of us jump into her arms. She isn't strong enough to lift us up. My father hands my mother her coat.

What I remember from that drive back is our life being turned upside down. Our father a changed man. We made a fuss of our mother. We brought her breakfast in bed. But that wasn't enough. She wanted to leave. To leave him. To leave everything behind.

This meant selling everything we had to sell and splitting the proceeds in two. Like cutting an apricot in half and throwing away the stone. This house, which was supposed to engrave our family story in stone, would instead become its tomb.

I insisted on being there every time one of the estate agents dealing with our bankruptcy came to visit the house. My mother and I were there for the first one. It was a very quick visit. I followed the two of them into each room. I wanted to point out each detail, tell the estate agent about each improvement my father had made, tell him how much we loved that house and that something that is loved should have more value.

I didn't say anything. The man only asked about the number of rooms and the size of each one, the south-facing windows, the house across the street, as if everything could be stated in terms of square metres and how many bathrooms it had.

We went back down to the living room. He sat at the dining table. He put his black leather briefcase on the oleander-patterned tablecloth. He took out a gold-coloured fountain pen, an accounting calculator and a blank page on which he scrawled a few numbers. He looked concerned, muttered figures to himself, one after another, tapped the buttons of his calculator, and then looked satisfied with the result.

He turned to my mother, who had lit a cigarette. She had been deliberately blowing smoke in his face while he was doing his calculations. He inhaled one last cloud of her contempt before proudly announcing the price of our life: 2,656,000 francs.

He sounded like a salesman, describing a bargain. My head was spinning. After we'd sold the house,

I thought, my parents would be rich. This was not the case.

My mother said: 'We have to tell your father.' I announced the sum as if telling him that we'd won the lottery. He took the news coldly. I had just told him his worth. His value as a man was this house.

The visits went on for several weeks, and then we sold the house. My father went his own way and my mother took us to her mother's house.

Time split in two. My mother's, and ours, continued moving forward. My father's stopped where it was, as if he'd left his soul in the house, taking only his rage with him.

In my paternal grandmother's garden, there was a double swing. There was a little yellow plastic basket with seats on either side, facing each other. My sister and I were placed in those seats.

We took it in turns to lean back, driving the swing ever higher. There was a safety device to stop the swing going over the top. A piece of plastic that made a big smacking noise every time we touched it.

The game was to be the first one to make the plastic smack. My parents' separation was a bit like that game, and my mother won: she made the swing smack first.

I never really knew what happened. I seem to remember that we were coming back from a weekend at my father's place. When we got home, there was a peculiar smell. The smell of my mother in moments like that. A smell that hit me in the throat and that I'd learned to recognise as soon as I opened the door – a stale odour mingling cigarette smoke, alcohol and warm sheets.

It soaked into walls and fabrics, it entered your sinuses and wouldn't leave, then it travelled down to your stomach and made you want to throw up, to run away. It was the smell of a life in decomposition.

My father throws us out of his car, then speeds away. A few moments later, he comes back. He rings the doorbell and my mother shouts from her bedroom: 'Don't let him in.' In the end, he jumps over the gate that I wish was covered with barbed wire and sharpened spikes. He walks to the door and bangs on it so hard that we feel the floor shake.

He paces around the house and stands in front of the kitchen window. Our eyes meet but I realise that he hasn't really seen me. He is looking through

me. I am transparent. Just another step on the staircase that will take him to what he wants.

I want to still love him. He calls out my name.
He says it in a gentler voice, like the wolf in the
Grimm fairy tale; I am one of the seven young goats.
He asks me to open the front door, tells me that
'Mummy' asked him to come. My mother keeps
yelling at me not to let him in.

I am merely an echo chamber. They are talking
through me. My father keeps walking around the
house, looking for an unlocked door, a half-open
window. He bangs on the bay window. My mother
orders me to close the shutters. All of them.

Heart pounding, I run as far away from him as I
can and start closing the shutters. There are so many
windows and so many shutters. It seems to take forever
to close them all. The house is almost in darkness. I
can hear my father's voice, muffled, begging my
mother from the garden. Telling her that he loves her
and needs her. And, in the same breath, telling her
that he hates her, that she has betrayed him.

I come to the last shutter. My father stands in
front of it. I put my hand around the crank handle
and observe him. He is silent. He leaves me to my

task. After all, I am alone with this choice. It is not a choice between him and her. That day, I chose the time in which I wanted to live.

I begin to turn the handle. Like a condemned man whispering his last wishes to his executioner, my father tells me it's not my fault. Then the guillotine falls. The shutters of my childhood close on that image of my discarded father. He will never have another life, only the memory of the one from which I have now excluded him.

The room is in almost total darkness now. A darkness so black that you have the impression you can see everything clearly. As if nothingness were impossible, and this impossibility inevitably produces light.

Today, for the first time, I imagine my father behind those shutters. I imagine him hating himself, hating the anger inside him. For the first time, I understand it and forgive it.

I understand the abandonment he felt, his fragility. I remember now that my father was loving and loved. And that he could never live without that love.

I inherited this quest for the absolute. This condemnation to failure. Deep down, our sorrows are repeated. We are imprisoned in the same way, because neither he nor I was able to live differently.

I forgive him now for relieving me of that burden. I come from that, from him. And, despite everything, I loved him. I am my father's son. His story – a part of his story – belongs to me now.

In the months that followed, my father settled into his suffering. He made his nest there. There were comings and goings. After the separation, like a vulture circling a dying love, my father listened out for the cry for help that my mother would give every time her life weighed too heavily on her, then he would land next to the carcass and wait.

He was there whenever my mother wasn't feeling well, which was pretty often. There was something broken in her, something that could not be fixed. She was a smashed glass and we kept cutting our feet on her because nobody wanted to sweep up the scattered shards.

The problem with bipolar disorder is that it leaves you with a glimmer of hope. Every time my mother returned, her boots still filthy with the dark earth of her depression, her features drawn after that exhausting journey, a new life began again. She acted as if she had never been away, as if she had never come back, as if all those days she spent in bed with a bottle of gin had never existed. She spoke to us, to my father, as if our lives had stopped at the same time hers had, and she was right. Our lives stopped and then they hung in suspension, waiting for the next relapse.

Those suspended moments had the same lightness as the start of the holidays. My mother put on make-up in the bathroom. She applied Rouge Coco to her thin lips. A line of mascara on her eyelashes, which opened to reveal irises as emerald and translucent as a mountain river on a spring morning. She was beautiful. She ran her fingers through her hair, her scarlet-painted nails matching perfectly with her strawberry-blonde curls.

She had an open smile and her heels tap-tap-tapped against the floor with a busy woman's cadence. We didn't worry about anything. Days passed. There was no more yelling in the evenings.

Then one day we went home and there was that stale smell. The television was on. My mother had dropped us at school then returned home. She had removed her Rouge Coco and her emerald eyes. She had opened a bottle of gin and had hidden little stores of it throughout the house. She'd stocked up on antidepressants. She'd lain down.

Try as I might, I can't remember the taste of my mother's kisses. I don't remember her smell, her warmth. I don't remember how it felt when she hugged us.

Will it be the same way for my son? When I recall the tenderest moments of my childhood, I think about my pyjamas.

That day, I realise that Melvil will never know his grandfather or grandmother. They were taken by their own tragedies, to which we children were mere spectators.

In 2005, my mother went off on one of her regular depressive cycles. She mixed alcohol and pills. She fell asleep with her cigarette still lit. The bed caught fire.

She was so numbed by the antidepressants, the sleeping pills and the gin that she couldn't move. She was burned alive, incapable of saving herself.

She didn't die immediately. She was taken to hospital and the doctors told us that she had suffered

95% burns. Only her face was intact; the rest of her body was black under the bandages.

We weren't able to talk to her. The doctors promised us that she wasn't in pain and we pretended to believe them.

I remember the muffled sound of the machines in her room. My last moments with her were spent looking through glass – as with my father, standing behind that window.

Then one evening my sister called me: the doctors had informed her that our mother was probably going to die that night.

'Do you want to come?'

I didn't go. I wasn't brave enough.

I stayed in Hélène's arms and I traded my anger for love.

I did all I could to forget the circumstances of her death and accept its reality.

I remember this line from my first book: 'Death awaited his mother that night; [the killers] were merely ambassadors.' And I understand where that line came from, and I think: it is true, too, for my mother. Melvil and I share the same scar.

I don't know how much time has passed. Maybe a minute, maybe ten. I can't hear Melvil any more, and I can't hear the anger either.

I open the door. He's standing in exactly the same spot where I left him. Mouth closed. Eyes wide open. I don't say anything, but I'm sorry.

I take off his jacket, his shoes, his trousers. I take off my shoes too.

We lie on the bed together. He takes my face and presses it against his. I'd like him to tell me that I didn't do anything wrong. That everything's all right.

He turns on his side, closes his eyes and falls asleep with a sigh.

The storm of ghosts left us washed up in this bed, the shutters closed.

8

September 2018

We were the first to arrive. My brother texted me the directions: 'It's the same hospital where Papa died. When you get to the lobby, keep going along the corridor straight ahead. There'll be lifts to your left and you'll go up to the third floor. We'll be waiting for you there.'

It's the end of the summer holidays. The air is getting lighter. The sun is still there, but it's more discreet, particularly in the mornings and evenings. In the daytime, we don't hide from it any more; we face up to it. It no longer beats down on us.

On the way there, we went past the house again. It was only a few minutes away from the hospital.

It looks much better in the September light. The shutters are closed.

It is not inhabited, but it seems alive all the same. The garden grows wild. You can imagine the boiler purring away inside, waiting for its masters' return. There's a leaking tap that they'll have to take care of when they get back. Smiles gathering dust on a bedside table will shine brightly again as soon as somebody looks at them.

No sound emerges from the house. Not my mother's groans or my father's yells. Not the dog's barks or the crestfallen faces of my sister and me. What does that sound like? It sounds like crestfallen faces. A deep, muffled sound. But here, there's only silence.

A few birds chirping, a lawnmower humming in the distance. No trace remains of our presence there. My ghosts have left this place for good. They have found a face, an identity, a refuge in my home. Our home.

My brother and my sister stayed in this area. At first I took this for cowardice, a lack of ambition, a narrow-mindedness on their part. To grow up, become an adult, to get old and die in the place where you were born struck me as the destiny of someone who had no sense of destiny.

I didn't understand how they could want to stay there, close to the old house, how they could accept the idea of not writing their own story, somewhere else.

We sometimes fought about this. They could sense my aversion for that life and they reproached me for going there to lecture them on their failings then disappearing on a sudden impulse. They were angry with me for casually throwing out everything that they'd patiently ordered, sorted through, tidied away.

For a long time I felt misunderstood, and then I realised that the misunderstanding was mine. That my brother and sister had moved forward, there, while I had fled.

Today, I can see the lost time and I don't regret any of those seconds spent far from myself. Today, I can see the time that's left and I want to join them there where they're waiting for me.

We reach the car park. Nothing has changed and yet it is no longer the same place. My first visit to this hospital was back at the time of my grandmother's death. My father's mother. She was walking home from her sister's house, carrying her handbag, and she just collapsed onto a grass verge by the roadside. A ruptured aneurysm. They asked us children if we wanted to see the body. I was surprised by that, at first. That we would be allowed to see a dead body. The only corpses I'd ever seen were on TV. I vividly remembered Laura Palmer's dead body on *Twin Peaks*. So I imagined my grandmother lying naked on her back, her skin bluish and her wet hair pushed back from her face. I imagined the smell of her decomposing body.

I said I wanted to go and see her. My grandmother was neither naked nor blue. Her hair wasn't wet. There was no particular smell in her room. No sombre music had been composed to soundtrack the moment when I discovered her dead body.

She was just lying there. Her body wasn't cold and her skin was still pinkish. The rings around her eyes were a little greyer than usual but she hadn't really changed. I stayed with her for a moment. I thought how few things separated us. A few ounces of oxygen, a few pints of blood, a few internal mechanics that had ceased to function. It struck me that the border between life and death was quite easy to cross.

One day, I thought, that will be me. But it was okay, because she looked fine. It didn't seem too serious.

*

It's a modern building constructed around an old building. In a few steps, you pass from one era to another. From the air-conditioned, sterilised, glass-walled lobby to a darker corridor, the small white floor tiles enlivened with a few hints of dark brown.

Melvil takes my hand as we enter an enormous lift that makes some disturbing sounds. He's wearing shorts and sandals. He has a holiday tan and his mouth is full of jokes.

I tell him to press the button for the third floor. When the doors slide open, my brother is standing there with a smile that goes all the way up to his eyes. I kiss his cheeks and hug him as tightly as I can, until he gives a little moan to signal that that's enough. His shoulders are slumped, his back slightly bent. He looks dejected and smells of the day before. He's tired, suddenly older, as if he has passed, overnight, from one age to another.

He leans down painfully to hug Melvil, who strokes his beard. This is a sign of recognition between the two of them. He hasn't aged that much, in fact; he is still young enough to be my little brother. The one we worried about. The unpredictable one. The one who was always getting into trouble. The one I went to fetch from the police

station when my father didn't feel up to it. The one
I put down in order to make myself feel better. The
one who forgave me for all that. The one holding
us all together. The point of convergence for the
telluric forces that shook our family.

There is nothing between us now but the joy of
seeing each other again. He leads us through a
corridor to the reception area. His wife is sitting
there. She looks exhausted, her features drawn. I
kiss her and tell her that I forgot to bring her present.
I always forget presents. I buy them long in advance
so I won't get caught out this time, then when the
day comes, I've forgotten all about them. I end up
giving them a few weeks or months later when their
impact is lost.

I whisper that I was thinking about her, that I
care about her. She pulls a small plastic box on wheels
towards me and says: 'Mia, I would like you to meet
your Uncle Antoine and your cousin Melvil.'

Mia is asleep. She's as red as a cherry. Her cheeks
are like apricots. Her head is cone-shaped. As if
there were a little party hat growing inside her skull.
Mia's mouth is pink and her legs are curled up. She
weighs six pounds and two ounces.

I was seven years old when my brother was born. At the hospital, my father offered to let me hold him in my arms. I refused. I said I was afraid of breaking him. He looked so fragile. So precious. So heavy. A baby weighs as much as the promise he carries. A promise of peace, renewal, eternity.

The only baby I held without hesitation was Melvil. I don't believe in instinct, whether paternal or maternal. I think, for me, it was a question of awareness: I was instantly aware of my responsibility, aware of the fact that Hélène and I were the only ones who could protect this defenceless little being, that I couldn't just slip away.

I am scared when she is placed into my arms. Scared that I have forgotten what to do. But it comes back to me straight away. I ask how the birth was, in the voice of someone who has already been through it before.

Caesarean or not? How long was the labour? In a softer voice, I ask: Episiotomy? Forceps? I gather information about the first hours after the birth. How did she sound when she cried? Did breast-feeding go well? Do you have a private room?

I go over everything. I take my time observing Mia. An entire life.

*

I remember it was a few days after the birth. We had gone back home: Hélène, Melvil and me. I was sitting on the sofa and he was lying in my arms, sucking on the bottle of formula that I was feeding him. Hélène was in the kitchen, just behind us. We talked for a while and then I fell silent. I could feel something rising inside me, although I didn't know what it was or why it was happening at that particular moment.

I started to cry. I couldn't stop. I was thinking about my mother, about my father, about Melvil and Hélène. Melvil immediately stopped drinking. He stopped until I had finished crying, then went back to his lunch.

He gave me time to cry. In truth, he has given me more than enough time. Enough time for me to cry my heart out. Enough time for my tears to dry up. He gave me time to cry and I used it for other things: to write, to go out, to have fun with him. We did so many things together. We thought: it's okay. We thought: let's go out. We thought: life goes on.

We went to the park. We went to the aquarium. We went to the zoo. We went to the funfair. We went to the woods of my childhood. We went to my old house. We went to the place where she and

I met. We went to my mother's grave again. We took the time to cry. We gave ourselves time to cry our hearts out. For our tears to dry up. We reconciled ourselves to time, to memory, to our story. We thought: we are adventurers and we are on another adventure.

Melvil asks me to put her down. He tells me that Mia is not coming to live with us. No, I agree, before pointing out that, one day, perhaps, he will have a little brother or sister of his own.

We go with my brother to grab a coffee. As we say goodbye, we make plans to do stuff together – holidays by the sea, looking after each other's kids – that will probably never come to fruition. Just saying it is enough, somehow; as if we've already experienced these things together.

My sister arrives just then. She has no time for us. She wants to see the baby. My brother asks for a bit more time. Just long enough to finish smoking the cigarette he's just lit. The three of us sit there without speaking. As we did in the hospital waiting room, wondering if we would get to see our mum. As we did when our dad was in a coma and we wondered if he would ever come out of it. As we did at my apartment on the night of 13 November when we wondered if Hélène would ever come home.

For a long time, we tried to resist all this. The three of us were united against adversity. Not any more. Now, we accept the blows of fate, the regrets and weaknesses, we let it break us, we bow down beneath its weight. We accept our family name. We bear it.

We kiss goodbye. On the way home, I tell Melvil about his first days of life, at the hospital. The first bath I gave him, in a sink. The beauty of his mother when she was tired. I tell him how his aunt and uncle came to see us and how beautiful they thought he was. How I wished his grandfather and grandmother could have seen him.

Lastly, I tell him that we will find their photographs when we get home, so I can show him what they looked like. His father's mother. His father's father.

9

January 2019

She is elegant. Her body is like a knife blade. She has long, slender legs that seem to bend backwards. An iridescent complexion. A slightly rounded belly.

I have always loved bellies. They're like little echo chambers. I love pressing my ear to them to hear the warmth, putting my mouth to them to taste the life gurgling inside.

Only a few months after meeting, we have made the decision to live together. It all happens very quickly. She is beautiful. Incredibly beautiful. She has an intelligence that sets us against each other, lifts us up, enriches our lives, and leaves us exhausted. And a gentleness too, that science of the softly placed hand, that art of sliding herself into the hollow of my collarbone, that need to be reassured.

That morning, it's the end of summer. She is returning from a holiday abroad. We go to the airport to fetch her. Melvil is happy to see her again. His smile and my words tell her that our apartment is ready to welcome her.

In the car, we tell each other about our holidays. It's a way of forgetting the apprehensiveness of the moment when we will have to go through the front door. That instant when 'us' will overshadow 'me', relegating it to a secondary role, a subplot, a backdrop.

This territory, which I have carefully pacified, must now adapt to the sudden appearance of a stranger. *Us* no longer means the two of us – Melvil and me mixed up together in a double-me. From now on, *us* will mean the three of us. A disparate collective, exploding our geography, giving each of us our 'me' back, and forcing those three *me*s to live together.

I dread the possibility that this won't work. It feels simultaneously like an invasion and a liberation. It's going to be difficult, I think, it's going to be hard, and probably quite testing, but we will get through it.

I feel contradictory emotions rising quickly inside me, but in the end it all comes down to a single truth: as she walks through the doorway into the apartment, I feel good. At the same time, I visualise the imprisonment that Melvil and I will not be able to escape. I breathe out. I see things anew. This woman will enable us to look beyond ourselves, to make a place in the world for us.

Loving, after. The question of desire after death is probably the most complex of all to examine, the most difficult to admit. You have to accept your weaknesses, accept that the child inside you, confronted with the most terrible abandonment, is going to cry and fuss until he calms down again.

In my case, I quickly felt a need for that presence. I needed the love that had become so familiar for me. I didn't see how I could live without it. Like my father, it seemed inconceivable to me, a life without loving. So I loved.

At first I called women I'd known before. I spread my feelings among all of them. I was so tired, and I had so much to think about. With hindsight, I think they sensed my distress and wanted to console me.

There were several before her. She was so different to the others. She wasn't attached to what I had been. I immediately wanted her close to me. I wanted us to be together, to be one.

With her, I no longer said: 'I don't want to be alone, I need someone.' Instead, I thought: 'I am going to love her. I am going to love her wounds and her contradictions. I am going to admire her intelligence. I am going to savour her presence.'

In the apartment, her first movements disturb our calm. They are jerky, disordered. The way she walks is slightly off balance, like all the women I have loved, a gait that betrays her uncertainty. She knocks into everything, overturns everything, without hesitation or equivocation. And, in this way, she hits me with the fact that I am still alive, that my life is not behind me.

I live through months of intense happiness. Complicated, but intense. Then something rises up inside me. A refusal, a faint anger towards her. It takes me a while to see it, to identify it, and yet it gets into everything, forming the words: 'You aren't part of that life.'

It's the weekend. The day before, I worked out our schedule: aquarium in the morning, then lunch outside on a restaurant terrace, then shopping for dinner. On Saturday, I offer to let her be part of these events, as if it is some privilege I am granting her. The privilege of being with us. As if that in itself was more than anybody could ask for.

I see disappointment on her face. And yet she is used to this. She suggests we go to the Louvre in the afternoon to visit the Egyptian exhibition. In other words, that I adapt my schedule for her. I know she is fascinated by ancient Egypt. She tells me about a radio programme that she heard a few days before.

I look tired before she even starts speaking. Melvil takes advantage of this to insinuate his way into a crack of silence in our conversation. I listen to the two of them at the same time. I try to balance things. I give her half of my attention, all that remains.

I end up refusing her suggestion about the Louvre; we won't have time, she should have told me earlier. My bad faith gets the upper hand, or perhaps it protects me from what would be too hard to face. She leaves, and slams the door behind her. With an embarrassed smile, I tell Melvil: 'Ready to go?' Deep down, I think: 'She takes up too much space.'

Before she moved in, I took some stuff out of drawers, little knick-knacks that could be kept in other places; small, unimportant things. When I realised that this wouldn't be enough, I cleared yet more space for her.

I brooded over this, without understanding that nothing would be enough. In the weeks and months that followed, there were other scenes. They were never violent, but they all told the same story. She wasn't dealing with one person, but two. Not a man with a child, but an inseparable whole.

Melvil and I were a planet and we allowed her to orbit around us, like a satellite. We left her in this discomfort until I felt an anger towards this foreign body. I became cruel. I made her pay for something that I hadn't yet identified by showing her that I could be cowardly, vile, insincere.

One evening, she told me she was leaving. I feigned indifference and felt relief. In the weeks after this, I went to her apartment several times to pick up my belongings, I didn't care about those belongings, I was simply incapable of dealing with grief again, however symbolic it might have been.

Even when there were no more belongings to pick up, I kept going to her apartment. I told her I understood, that I was going to change. In the end, I begged her to come back. When she finally did, I was so happy. I called everyone I knew and told them I was going to have more children.

We made love. Then I hurt her again. For no reason. I was like those kids who pull the legs off insects to see if they can still walk. I had so much anger.

When a love is born and when it dies, there is always a strange moment of confusion. Something hard to describe. A sort of interim period. A purgatory. A time of adaptation during which your body, unsure what it wants to welcome or reject, leaves your mind in a suspended state.

What, just before, seemed impossible, suddenly becomes perfectly feasible, because that moment of uncertainty is shared, because neither of you really knows, because both of you are waiting for the moment to decide things for you.

The moment made its decision. Or perhaps it was that unconquerable anger inside me. She left me alone with Melvil. Once again, I had to protect my son from loss.

That week, I receive a message from my friend Michel, a lifebelt thrown to a drowning man. He invites us to go with him to Brittany for a few days, to the place where he grew up.

It's a beautiful day. We all catch the sun, even though it's covered by clouds. It's windy too – a wind that carries you rather than pushing you back. A tall, talkative blonde woman welcomes us into the house where we'll be staying. She's a friend of Michel's. A good friend: she was the one who told him he had the right to become a DJ, to love boys, and to leave.

The house is big and she still hasn't finished renovating it – she probably never will. We are given a small studio apartment on the ground floor. If we stand on tiptoe, we can see the sea. Sitting on my shoulders, Melvil has an even better view.

One day, we set off for the end of the world. In Brittany, each B-road exit leads to an end of the world. We stop at a beach to make sandcastles. Melvil leads us up a small, rocky path. At the top, we find ourselves on a large cliff overlooking the sea. An elderly lady with knotted hands and a worried look in her eyes seems to be waiting for us there, in her garden.

Michel immediately recognises Monique. She ran the nightclub where he spent his happiest summers. Sixteen years old, surrounded by boys, dancing to Whitney Houston. She urges us into her wooden house, which looks like a ship run aground.

Cardboard boxes, books and other belongings are scattered all over the place, but everything is there. The dance floor is intact, and so are the lights, the sound equipment, the bar and the barrels on which they used to sit and drink. Michel points out the DJ booth – a small, square box, a throne for the king of the night.

Melvil does not say a word. He listens, fascinated. All day long, he never questions anything. The long waits in restaurants for ham-and-cheese crepes that he has no desire to eat. The miles in a car. The long coastal walks.

There's a family anecdote about me. I was a very quiet little boy. I didn't speak. I listened to the grown-ups. One day, at a restaurant, I was so silent that they forgot I was there and almost left me behind. But since the day I started speaking, I have never stopped. I even made it my job, by becoming a radio journalist. Melvil is that little boy too; he knows when he can be a child and when he should follow the adults.

On our last morning, Michel has to work. Since Melvil and I have the morning to ourselves, we take our time waking up and getting dressed, before going out to buy a chocolate croissant. Melvil wants to eat it on the beach, just below the house. He's brought his bucket and spade with him to make sandcastles. We put our bare feet in the icy water, dig holes to bury our bad memories.

The sun and the clouds divide up their territory, leaving us under a piebald sky. It's springtime and Melvil is wearing a jumper with a drawing of a fire engine on it. It's not too hot, not too cold. The air is still and the sea grey.

From time to time, we see people walk past in wetsuits, submerged in water up to their waist. They move as if in slow motion. Melvil asks me who these strange people are. I tell him they must be searching the sea for something they've lost.

I wonder what we are searching for.

*

Melvil comes and sits next to me. He's finished his sandcastle, trampled it into the ground, built it again and trampled it again, and now he's had enough. He asks me when we're going to see Michel again. 'Soon,' I tell him.

'Are you enjoying your holiday?'

'Yes.'

I tell him we came on holiday not far from here with Mama once, when he was a baby. We rented a car to make the trip. I tell him he was so young that he spent the nights sleeping beside us in a Moses basket. We put the mattress on the floor so we'd be at the same height as him. We were bitten by spiders all night.

At the end of the garden, there was a cliff and – fifteen or twenty metres below – a beach that looked almost exactly like the one where we are now. I remember the wind, blowing so hard that it seemed to knock on the door. I open that door and recall the first summer in Paris that we spent together, inside each other, inseparable. How beautiful Hélène was. Our little June baby who had a growth spurt every summer.

Anger gives way to love. I remember it at last. I let myself remember it. How much I loved her.

Hélène wasn't an excuse or a fantasy. I didn't know how to love before I met her.

I never knew and I still don't know how it was made, that visceral attachment we felt, that almost brother–sister closeness, that desire for each other and to be with each other that never faded, never withered, never shrank. I know that I wanted her instantly, entirely. I wanted her to be mine. To have and to hold.

To start with, she said no. That was the first evening. We kissed like teenagers then she put her hand on mine to stop me. She said she wouldn't be mine. She wasn't teasing me or playing hard-to-get. It wasn't a strategy. What she meant was: that is not the desire that I will receive. That is not the urge that will create this love.

I say love because I have no other word to define what is undefinable. I never knew and still don't know how we found that balance where our desires could meet without conflicting, without one getting the upper hand over the other, without either of us getting hurt.

I never knew and I still don't know how to describe that state of plenitude and grace, or that anxiety in the face of loss, that feeling of not being yourself any more, of being surpassed by another, the need to measure up to them. I abandoned myself to that love. I had never been so free. I had never been so beautiful. I wanted her arms, her belly, her mouth, her voice. I wanted her past, her future, her presence.

'Do you remember those holidays?' I ask Melvil. A few months ago, even a few weeks ago, he wouldn't have said anything. This time, instead of turning away, he stares at me as if wanting to hear more about them.

For the past four years, I have regularly talked to Melvil about his mother. She has become the words spoken by the people who knew her: her mother, her sister, her friends, and me. Melvil listens and sometimes he recites what he's heard, but there is never a conversation.

I tell him about her, but I don't mention the circumstances of her death. Not directly. You can't tell a child: your mother is dead – you must weep for her, and then we'll be able to reconstruct an image and a story based on that. He will ask about her death himself, when the time is right.

*

A year after Hélène's death, I called a friend who'd lost her husband at the same time; her son is three or four years older than Melvil. She was in the car when she took my call, with her phone on loudspeaker.

The first thing that the boy asked when he heard my voice was: 'Is that Papa on the phone?'

Children wait for the dead to return. Grief is nothing more or less than this long wait until acceptance. When the waiting ends, then they will weep. The waiting protects them, keeps them alive, until they understand that the dead never come back.

On the advice of a child psychiatrist, I waited too. I waited for the moment when Melvil would start asking questions. I knew it could take years, but I waited with him. I put everything to one side, out of sight, while we waited for the right moment.

It probably suited me, to some extent. On the beach, I look at Melvil and think about the time, years before, when I went to visit my uncle after my mother's death.

I visit him because I need to talk about her. He's my father's brother, but he knew my mother, and I'd like him to tell me what he knows. I want to find out what films she watched, what music she listened to, the cafés where she used to go. A trace, a taste, a detail, anything that might give me a glimpse of her lost substance.

That day, it's February, and the sky is dark early. I take him a bottle of Japanese whisky. Drinking loosens the tongue. Whisky especially. I go into his house, at the back of a small street in Ivry-sur-Seine. The layout is quite haphazard. There's a games room at the end of the kitchen, and the bedrooms are scattered along a corridor that runs through the main building to the extension.

My uncle wears a wise expression. He is gentle and he leads me into his living room. He signals for me to take a seat in one of the large leather armchairs. He asks me about my job as a radio journalist. I tell him about the apartment where Hélène and I have moved, on rue Cadet in the ninth arrondissement.

My uncle smiles with his eyes. Even as a little boy, I admired him. He lived in Burkina Faso back then. Whenever he came back to France, during the summer holidays, he would look like an explorer, with his rumpled white shirt, the buttons undone, and his canvas trousers. It was my uncle who showed me how travelling could make existence bearable.

In his living room, I am struck by how different he is to my father. He seems joined, slow, linear, where my father is twitchy. My uncle gives the impression of a man whose destiny has been fulfilled. The two brothers are like enemies, opposed in every way except that of their origin. They are like the brothers in Maupassant's novel *Pierre and Jean*: my uncle the fortunate Jean, my father the bitter Pierre, the first embodying the luminous side of the second.

He pours us each a glass of whisky. 'Do you want to tell me about Africa?' I ask him at last. He tells me what I already know. Then to keep the conversation going – like someone blowing on a fire that's going out – I tell him that I am working on a documentary adaptation of *Phantom Africa* by Michel Leiris – my great-great-uncle, a glorious ancestor who created an ethnographic travel journal about that continent.

I'd discovered him as a child when I was looking through an encyclopedia to see if my name was in it. I asked who this 'Michel Leiris' was. A writer, I was told, and a horrible man. Later, reading his autobiography, *Manhood*, I discovered that I was descended from his hated brother. I thought again about my uncle and my father. They, too, had fought at times and – as far as I could remember – it was always my uncle, the younger, who tried to make peace. The little brother who fled my father has remained.

The Leiris inheritance consists of warring brothers and silence. Both of those traits are mingled in me, to some degree.

The idea behind my adaptation of *Phantom Africa* was to recreate that journey in today's world. From Dakar to Djibouti, via all the moods and emotions that the voyage would provoke in me.

I wait for my uncle's approval. He is doubtful: 'It would be impossible, given the political situation.' He explains it to me: Islamisation, the colonial legacy. He talks a lot about space, until the conversation dies out.

We are both exhausted by this exchange. I had come to talk about my mother, but both of us are relieved to see the conversation end without mention of her name. We part on that silence, promising to meet up again soon.

It won't happen. Nor will I make Michel Leiris's voyage in reverse. Like my uncle and my famous ancestor, I will lock away the ghosts in Africa. My mother's ghost. My father's. And Hélène's. Over the past four years, I have only let her come to me once a year – on All Saints' Day, when I go to her grave, alone, to talk to her. When I go to her grave, alone, to take care of it.

I clean the stone. Carefully, and often in silence, as if – through the stone – it is her intact body that I am caring for once again.

The Jews have a tradition of washing the body of the dead before it is buried by the men of the family. When Hélène's father died in Tangiers, I flew there with Hélène and her sister. They weren't allowed to attend the funeral ceremony or the burial. They had to stand and wait at the cemetery gates, while I went inside on their behalf.

We take the same care for a gravestone as we do for the body of the dead. And those graves all around remind me that death is a story in itself, a story shared by all of us, the greatest common denominator.

The cemetery is one of those rare places where you never feel truly alone.

Melvil goes back to the sea with his rake, as if tactfully leaving me to continue a conversation that he feared he would interrupt.

I think he can sense a presence too, that he can tell I'm not alone here on the sand. There are three of us now.

The wind blows and, for the first time, I feel her there, around us.

No more anger, no more anything, just gusts of presence. Our mourning can begin.

'Yes,' I say, out loud. 'Look, he's growing up.' My phone rings – it's Michel. I ask him to give us a little longer. Soon after that, I call out to Melvil and wave him back to me and the three of us lie down, side by side.

Love, after. It's a ghosts' love. It means accepting that that particular love belongs to its ghost, but that another, different love can be born.

That evening, we go back to the little studio flat. I put Melvil to bed and begin writing this book. I want to describe this new period that led me to her.

I feel immensely alive. In front of my computer, I feel those presences around me. My father, my mother, Hélène. She appears in the room as soon as I type the first letter.

Her black hair falling halfway down her back. Her delicate hands showing the gentleness of her character. She has owl's eyes, which she has passed on to Melvil. He will see the world through his mother's eyes. Literally.

She sits at one end of the sofa. Discreetly, like someone who's just passing through. Seeing her sit there, just beside me, I realise it's been too long since I last looked at her.

I remember every detail of her features. For me, her beauty was always a mystery. A whole that I could never deconstruct. Something sensual and feminine, desirable and maternal, fragile and unshakeable.

More than once, I wanted to eat her. Her skin, her apple flesh, her sweet flavour. I wrote my first story and I devoured her, swallowed her, left nothing behind. I put her body on my pages and then I closed the book. What she'd stopped me doing twelve years earlier by placing her hand on mine, I had done behind her back, when she had no say in the matter, when she was no longer able to reason with me.

Now that our story has become a story, now that our characters can look after themselves, it is time to find her again.

*

Hélène is the pen that I hold, the ink flowing inside, the keyboard under my fingertips, the words that appear on the screen. The letters have her curves, the words her tact and sensitivity. The sentences echo with her musicality.

The epigraph of this book is a quote by Maurice Blanchot: 'Whoever wishes to remember must surrender to forgetfulness, to the risk of absolute oblivion and to that beautiful randomness which then becomes memory.' I found it in the opening pages of Jorge Semprun's *Literature or Life*.

Writing and life.

The memory of Hélène comes back to me. To write about her is to breathe life into her. To understand that she was there all along. In the background, hidden by the light, erased by the everyday, right there but no longer there, as she was behind that Plexiglas pane in the mortuary, the last time I saw her.

The next day, we drive back to Paris.

Melvil is in his car seat, behind me. The radio is on in the background. One of the latest hits, 'Tout Oublier' ('Forget Everything'), fills the inside of the car.

'*Doesn't exist without its opposite / And that seems easy to find.*'

I can see him listening. I turn up the volume.

'*Gotta forget everything / To believe, you gotta forget everything.*'

'Papa?'

'Yes?'

'What does that mean, forget everything?'

I think about this. It means that I thought everything could start again. I thought I could mark out a space and my regrets would stay in there. I thought I would be stronger than grief. That I could tame it.

It means that I thought it was too heavy a burden to bear. That I wanted us to feel lightened. It means that I took her away from us.

To explain words to a child, you have to rediscover their meaning.

'If you forget everything, it means you leave all the bad memories behind and you don't think about them any more.'

Forget. Forget. Like a chorus stuck in your head. I've done precisely what I didn't want to do. I forgot because, to believe, I had to forget everything.

'*Melancholy's gone out of fashion / Being happy isn't complicated / Melancholy's gone out of fashion / It's not complicated.*'

'What's fashion?'

I think about this. It's what was. What no longer is.

'Fashion is what everybody wants at the same time.'

'Why has melancholy gone out of fashion?'

EPILOGUE

The air is white. Through the open windows, we can hear sounds from outside. The apartment is quiet.

It's late June 2015 and Paris is in its last spasm of activity before falling asleep for the summer. There's something fascinating about the way this city sleeps. It becomes something else. Empty.

You can spot details that were hidden, before, by the crowds and the noise. There's the smell of hot stone, the light erasing perspective and crunching the city into a ball of paper. A gust of wind stirs the plane trees below and it sounds like the sea.

Hélène is tired. I like it when she's tired. There's a sort of anxiety in her eyes, as though she's on the alert.

I suggest she has a lie-down. Her body relaxes. It becomes elastic. You have to handle it with care.

I put Melvil down for his nap. He's just turned one. He observes this early afternoon spinning in slow motion. His eyes close of their own accord. He's a ball of cotton wool as I place him gently in his cot after changing his nappy. He exhales deeply. It's the sound that eternity must make.

I join her in bed, a sheet of paper in hand. I wedge some pillows behind my head so I can read more comfortably. She rests her head on my shoulder. Her lashes tickle my bare chest.

She's still wearing her T-shirt. I tell her I've decided to write a birthday letter to Melvil every year. I say that when he's an adult, I'll give them all to him so he can read and reread his life, fill in the gaps, and invent what happens next.

I wrote the first one in a few minutes on a corner of the table. She asks me to read it to her. I begin.

Melvil, my son, my love,

You're only one year old today but you're already so big. Barely a second ago, you were still a tiny little thing, just out of your mother's belly. Your face was all eyes — those big dark eyes that opened as soon as you began what is now your life.

I spent that first hour with you. You took your time coming out. Afterwards, you were a little tired and the doctors wanted to check that nothing was wrong. You fitted inside my hand. I told you that you would have a long and beautiful life.

It was 11 June 2014, very late in the evening. I will always remember the moment when the midwives placed you in your mother's arms. She burst into tears, overwhelmed by an emotion for which no word has yet been found.

So, to describe that simultaneous coexistence, in the space of an instant, of joy, fear, tenderness and vertigo, they invented love. Your mother and I fell in love the day you appeared.

Children must think that their parents have always been parents. It's not true: the second before your arrival, we were still the children of our parents. Ever since, we've just been trying to do our best. Your mother is perfect. I do what I can.

Right now, your father is at a crossroads in his life. To keep moving forward, he has to take risks. And he needs courage to take those risks.

Your mother is here with me, and she will always be there for you. If you ever have any doubts, she has — inside her — the confidence that will enable you to overcome them. And you are there, my angel, to protect me from the demons that assail me.

Discovering this letter four years later.

Rereading it, and understanding: those letters have become books. And Hélène, too, is still there.

You Will Not Have My Hate was not a betrayal. It was her, even then.

It's three in the afternoon. I get up from my desk. I have to pick up Melvil early from school because he has a doctor's appointment.

On the way there, I think about the other letters that I wrote for him. I think about the one where I tell him about his mother's death. I think about all the letters I haven't yet written.

I go through the gate. He's in the playground, but he doesn't look surprised to see me. I watch him getting down from the wooden lorry in the middle of that concrete yard.

He's just turned five. I hear him telling his friends: 'My papa's here.' He runs towards me. I see two little girls saying goodbye to him as he leaves. He smiles at them.

I feel a kind of joy, thinking that he has a life of his own. That he won't always be trapped inside mine. That he will grow up and love.

I enter the school, carried along on a wind of pure happiness. I kiss the little monkey that wraps itself around me. No, I don't kiss it, I eat it. He pushes me away and climbs down from his palm tree.

Thinking that he has a life of his own and that it's just begun.

Mine, too, has started again. The ghosts have found their place. They are no longer roaming my mind, no longer haunting our home. They are part of our family.

THE LEOPARD

The leopard is one of Harvill's historic colophons and an imprimatur of the highest quality literature from around the world.

When The Harvill Press was founded in 1946 by former Foreign Office colleagues Manya Harari and Marjorie Villiers (hence Har-vill), it was with the express intention of rebuilding cultural bridges after the Second World War. As their first catalogue set out: 'The editors believe that by producing translations of important books they are helping to overcome the barriers, which at present are still big, to close interchange of ideas between people who are divided by frontiers.' The press went on to publish from many different languages, with highlights including Giuseppe Tomasi di Lampedusa's *The Leopard*, Boris Pasternak's *Doctor Zhivago*, José Saramago's *Blindness*, W. G. Sebald's *The Rings of Saturn*, Henning Mankell's *Faceless Killers* and Haruki Murakami's *Norwegian Wood*.

In 2005 The Harvill Press joined with Secker & Warburg, a publisher with its own illustrious history of publishing international writers. In 2020, Harvill Secker reintroduced the leopard to launch a new translated series celebrating some of the finest and most exciting voices of the twenty-first century.

Laurent Binet: *Civilisations*
    trans. Sam Taylor
Paolo Cognetti: *Without Ever Reaching the Summit*
    trans. Stash Luczkiw
Pauline Delabroy-Allard: *All About Sarah*
    trans. Adriana Hunter
Urs Faes: *Twelve Nights*
    trans. Jamie Lee Searle
Ismail Kadare: *The Doll*
    trans. John Hodgson
Jonas Hassen Khemiri: *The Family Clause*
    trans. Alice Menzies
Karl Ove Knausgaard: *In the Land of the Cyclops: Essays*
    trans. Martin Aitken
Karl Ove Knausgaard: *The Morning Star*
    trans. Martin Aitken
Antoine Leiris: *Life, After*

trans. Sam Taylor

Geert Mak: *The Dream of Europe*

trans. Liz Waters

Haruki Murakami: *First Person Singular: Stories*

trans. Philip Gabriel

Haruki Murakami: *Murakami T: The T-Shirts I Love*

trans. Philip Gabriel

Ngũgĩ wa Thiong'o: *The Perfect Nine: The Epic of Gĩkũyũ and Mũmbi*

trans. the author

Intan Paramaditha: *The Wandering*

trans. Stephen J. Epstein

Per Petterson: *Men in My Situation*

trans. Ingvild Burkey

Dima Wannous: *The Frightened Ones*

trans. Elisabeth Jaquette